# Dinner can be equal parts impressive and simple any day of the week. Sometimes all you need is a little inspiration and a cabbage—and this book!

*A Generous Meal* is a modern cookbook of over 100 recipes that anyone, from a novice to an experienced chef like Christine, can use to whip up restaurant-quality meals with ease.

Christine Flynn shows us—contrary to popular belief—that you don't need a lot of time, money, or know-how to make good food. A simple potato can transform a so-so day into something special, a soup can warm you in more ways than one, and baking a chocolate cake is just another way of shouting, "I love you!" at the top of your lungs.

Maybe you are having people over and want to put out some crusty bread and serve an array of simple starters like Butter Beans in Salsa Verde or Warm Chorizo in Sidra that will get everyone nibbling. Or, perhaps you're looking for a vegetable-forward weeknight meal like Spicy Oven Charred Cabbage and Lemons. Seafood dishes, including Herb Stuffed Rainbow Trout and Cod and Zucchini in Curry Coconut Broth, offer good variety, and meaty mains like Crispy Chicken Thighs over Vinegar Beans or Lamb Loin Chops over Minty Pistachio Butter are perfect any day of the week—and just as impressive to serve to guests.

And what is a meal without the possibility of dessert? Satisfy your post-dinner sweet tooth cravings with recipes like Caramel Pecan Ice Cream Crumble Cake or Polenta Biscuits with Sweet Corn Cream and Strawberries.

The recipes in *A Generous Meal* are fresh, comforting, easy to follow, and the best part? They are enjoyable to cook *and* eat.

# A Generous Meal

# A Generous Meal

## Modern Recipes for Dinner

### Christine Flynn

PENGUIN

an imprint of Penguin Canada, a division of Penguin Random House Canada Limited

Canada • USA • UK • Ireland • Australia • New Zealand • India • South Africa • China

First published 2023

www.penguinrandomhouse.ca

Library and Archives Canada Cataloguing in Publication

Title: A generous meal : modern recipes for dinner / Christine Flynn.
Names: Flynn, Christine, 1983- author.
Identifiers: Canadiana (print) 20220142343 | Canadiana (ebook) 20220142351 |
ISBN 9780735241596 (hardcover) | ISBN 9780735241602 (EPUB)
Subjects: LCSH: Cooking. | LCSH: Dinners and dining. | LCGFT: Cookbooks.
Classification: LCC TX714 .F628 2023 | DDC 641.5/4—dc23

Cover and book design by Leah Springate and Matthew Flute
Cover and interior photography by Suech and Beck
Food styling by Lindsay Guscott
Prop Styling by Andrea McCrindle

Printed in China

10 9 8 7 6 5 4 3 2 1

Penguin
Random House
PENGUIN CANADA

For my daughters, again.
And for Denise, who has
always been a believer.

# Contents

# A Centre of Vegetables

# Delicious Fishes Dishes

# Meat the Mains

# Just Desserts

# Condiments and Other Necessary Recipes

# Introduction

Dinner, for me, is the most important meal of the day. When shared with friends or family, it is an opportunity to bring people together over delicious food and good conversation. Eaten alone, dinner can be a restorative break in what is sometimes a chaotic life, especially when you prepare exactly the thing you want to eat in exactly the way you want to eat it. In either case, dinner is a meal worth lingering over.

*A Generous Meal* is a cookbook (with essays) that is meant to improve your life. I want to show you that you don't need a lot of time, a lot of money, or a lot of know-how to make good food. You can, without too much effort, feed yourself very well with a cabbage and some inspiration (page 147). Even after decades of cooking (and eating), I still find it incredible how little is required to be kind to yourself and to others and how easy it is to create a thoughtful, nourishing meal.

My hope is that this book will make cooking and eating dinner more enjoyable for you, and something you look forward to as a way to take care of yourself and the people around you. I do not want the time you spend in the kitchen to feel laborious or like a chore. Life is too short to do things that make you unhappy.

Whether you are new to cooking or have been whipping up good things in the kitchen for decades, this book will show you the potential of everyday ingredients and, in doing so, also show you the potential of every day. Whether you are craving the bright acidity and familiar flavours found in a dish like Caesar Beans (page 57) or something a bit richer and a little different like Crispy Potatoes over Creamy Tonnato (page 86), you will find recipes that are craveable but also so straightforward you will want to make them again and again. I have included as many vibrant, mouthwatering vegetable-centred recipes as are in my current repertoire, such as Spicy Oven Charred Cabbage and Lemons (page 152) and Roasted Delicata Squash and Feta with Hot Honey (page 141), but since I am unabashedly an omnivore, there are also meatier recipes like Harissa Chicken (page 213) and Pan Seared Ribeyes with Ramp and Anchovy Butter (page 241) and fishier recipes like Herb Stuffed Rainbow Trout (page 200) and Eggs and Lobster Baked in Cream (page 188). Peppered throughout, you will find recommendations for what to eat together, such as Fried Cheese Salad (page 117) and Lamb Loin Chops over Minty Pistachio Butter (page 231) or some Warm Chorizo in Sidra with Charred Bread (page 38) paired with Roasted Butternut Squash with Labneh and Pistachios (page 138).

> **Baking someone a chocolate cake is just another way of shouting, "I love you!" at the top of your lungs.**

And, whether you are alone or together, what is a meal without the possibility of dessert? My daughters will tell you that something sweet completes dinner, and I will tell you that if I am making an additional course, it better be a snap to prepare—and preferably the sort of thing I can blitz in a blender, transfer to a cake pan, and *voilà*, as they say in France, *ze cake, she is done*. For this sort of simple but effective sweet ending, you must simply make a Torte in a Hurry (page 273) or perhaps a Plum and Black Pepper Clafoutis (page 265). If you feel the inclination and the urge, try making something a bit more complex like an Apple Tart with Rose Cream (page 267) or a Marble Cake (page 269), which has the sort of casual elegance that impresses everyone.

All writers are told, first and foremost, to write what they know, so the recipes here are just that. What I know is that a potato has the power to transform a so-so day into something special, that a soup can warm you in more ways than one, and that baking someone a chocolate cake is just another way of shouting, "I love you!" at the top of your lungs. So, please, get comfortable, pour yourself something lovely to drink, and enjoy *A Generous Meal*.

# Pantry Essentials

Since becoming a mother, I've made it a habit to keep a well-stocked pantry. Having babies, and later toddlers, meant that dashing out for a bottle of fish sauce or a lemon at 5:30 pm was a near-impossible feat and, in general, not one I wished to tackle. While your situation is no doubt different from mine, we can all benefit from having what we need within reach. Even if you don't always know what you are going to cook when the sun begins to set, keeping the essentials and a few smart condiments at the ready makes cooking more intuitive. As you use this book, you'll (hopefully!) build up your own stockpile of staples to cook with. Here is a list to get you started.

> Even if you don't always know what you are going to cook when the sun begins to set, keeping the essentials and a few smart condiments at the ready makes cooking more intuitive.

## Cupboard

**Extra-virgin olive oil**
You need one fancy extra-virgin olive oil for drizzling and one everyday, cheap and cheerful bottle for cooking.

**Walnut oil**
I call for this ingredient quite a bit because it adds not just fat to a dish but also a ton of flavour. Of all the nut oils, walnut is my favourite because it lends a subtle nuttiness wherever it lands, creating depth in a dish without being overpowering. Look for a cold-pressed oil and store it either in the fridge or in a cupboard away from heat sources like the stove, which will cause it to go rancid and taste bitter more quickly.

### Canola oil

I use a locally made cold-pressed canola oil. Unlike extra-virgin olive oil, it has a neutral flavour and can be used for sautéing, salad dressings, and even baking.

### White vinegar

For all-purpose vinegar, I reach for my giant, industrial-size jug of white vinegar. I use it to finish soups, brighten braises, double down on the acidity of my salads, and keep my pie crusts flakey. It has a clean flavour and is also easily infused with aromatics or blended with other acids for more complex flavour.

### Tahini

Oh, tahini, what can't it do? Tahini is a wonder-condiment. Smoosh it on toast with date syrup and sea salt for a quick snack; whip it with water, garlic, and lemon to make Tahini Dip (page 294); or swirl it into salad dressings for some creamy mouthfeel feelings. It's so good. Look for a well-made brand that tastes fresh, not bitter, and store it in a cool, dark place.

### Tinned fish

I have a whole shelf in my pantry dedicated to tinned fish. It can be an instant meal alongside some charred bread and hot sauce, or the beginning of a great dish like Trout Salad with Yogurt and Jammy Eggs (page 178). I keep a variety on hand, and it's one of those things I always buy when I see it at a specialty shop. My favourites are trout, cod, mackerel, small sardines, and mussels escabeche. It's not technically a fish, but tinned octopus is also delicious and looks extra impressive when you put it out on a snack board.

### Stock

I make stock when I can, but there's nothing wrong with the store-bought stuff. I would not use Campbell's Low Sodium Chicken Stock to make a consommé for the Queen, but to knock together a Sauerkraut Soup (page 129) on a Tuesday, it's just the ticket. I keep chicken stock for general purpose and usually one lonely Tetra Pak of beef stock that I use when I'm looking for a bolder, richer flavour from the cupboard. And because I have now experienced a global pandemic, I even have a jar of powdered chicken bouillon that I can use as a substitute for stock. It lasts forever and you can use it in a pinch to no great detriment.

### Beans and lentils

Canned and dried beans and lentils are so useful in creating nourishing, thoughtful meals. I keep a variety of lentils on hand, but the ones I reach for the most are red lentils and white lentils.

### Grains

When it comes to grains, I keep farro, freekeh, and both basmati and jasmine rice on hand. Store your grains and rice in nice big glass jars so you can see them to pull them out easily, and make sure you don't let them sit for too long. Like any ingredient, they can become stale.

### Spices

There is a whole world of spices out there, and even with years of cooking under my belt, I am still finding new ones I love. There is no reason to run out and buy all the spices, but continue to add to your collection as you need them.

The spices I use most often in this book, beyond salt and pepper, are Aleppo pepper, paprika, turmeric, cumin, and coriander. When possible, I buy small amounts of organic spices because I find the flavour to be fresher and more vibrant. To maximize their shelf life, keep your spices in containers with a tight seal and away from a heat source (so not in the cupboard above your stove). Don't forget to check them every few months, as spices can go stale like anything else. If a spice has gone off, you will notice it either has no smell at all or even a slightly rancid smell. When that happens, it's time to discard stale spices and get new ones.

### Baking essentials

What you really need to have on hand is all-purpose flour, granulated sugar, baking powder, and baking soda. And before you tell me you are not a baker, skip ahead to the desserts section and *just look* at how many very simple, quick recipes there are for cakes, bakes, and pies. Technically I'm not a baker either, but I do get a thrill from puréeing five things in a blender, popping the resulting batter in the oven, and pretending I am. None of the recipes in this book is overly complicated, and you really can make magic with these pantry staples.

# Fridge

**Fresh herbs**

If you like fresh herbs, boy are you going to love this book (page 199)! My go-to herbs are mint, parsley, dill, and basil. In the winter I buy them from the grocery store, and after a gentle rinse I wrap them loosely in a clean dish towel and store them in the fridge for up to a week or so. In the summer I plant herbs in my garden for an unending supply, and I simply snip as needed. I also like to plant edible flowers such as pansies, nasturtiums, and chrysanthemums, which I will toss into salads or even on top of a pizza for my daughters.

**Cheese**

When it comes to the cheeses I keep on hand, I follow what I like to call the Golden Rule: one hard, one soft, one goat or sheep. I like to keep a big wedge of pecorino, an aged hard cheese from Italy that is suitable for putting out on a board or grating into a Green Lasagna (page 167). Save the rinds of hard cheeses for slipping into brothy soups like Sauerkraut Soup (page 129) or even Brothy Farro with Mushrooms and Tofu (page 133). My soft cheese of choice is something munchable and meltable, like brie. You also might like Saint André or my absolute favourite, Brillat-Savarin. As for the goat or sheep component, I love manchego—especially drizzled with Hot Honey (page 293)—and funkier goat cheeses like Crottin de Chavignol.
I always buy the biggest containers of feta I can find—preferably Macedonian feta, which is creamier than Greek feta—and make sure the cheese is swimming in brine, as I use that too.

**Full-fat plain yogurt**

Is there anything worse than buying plain yogurt with the intention of adding it to Trout Salad with Yogurt and Jammy Eggs (page 178) or Steak Salad with Pepperoncini and Green Goddess Dressing (page 235) and getting it home only to discover that it's vanilla? You can put plain yogurt in loads of dishes to add creamy tang, or even serve it alongside a spicier dish to temper the heat. But if you buy vanilla yogurt by mistake, you're out of luck. Double-check the labels and, yes, always buy plain yogurt, full fat if possible.

**Pickles**

I make some pickles at home, but the crunch of a Bick's Kosher Style Dill is something I will never master, and that's totally okay. Keep on hand a mix of store-bought and homemade pickles like Bread and Butter Pickles (page 291), to serve in cute little dishes with toothpicks or for chopping to add to Tartar Sauce (page 295) or for slicing up for a sandwich. Use the pickling liquid to make new pickles or drizzle it over a salad for an extra kick of pickle-y acid.

### Fish sauce

I use fish sauce in places you would expect, such as in Cod and Zucchini in Curry Coconut Broth (page 195), but also in places you might not expect, such as in Caesar Beans (page 57) and Crispy Potatoes over Creamy Tonnato (page 86). Just a small amount of fish sauce adds big umami flavour—and depth of flavour that can really ground a dish. I love it, and I use it often and liberally!

# Freezer

### Fresh bread

I like to buy very good bread from the local bakery and cut it in half before I freeze it. Putting out a spread is a snap when you have some crusty bread that's taken a quick ride in a hot oven. Add a few pantry items drizzled in chili oil and a green salad, and off you go.

### Stale bread

Stale bread is a real workhorse in the kitchen. Soak it in milk for your meatballs, grind it into Bread Crumbs (page 289), toast it and put an egg on it, tear it into chunks for a Winter Panzanella Salad (page 121), bake it into a bread pudding, etc., etc. The lesson here is to keep your stale bread, and you will be presented with a million opportunities to use it.

### Lime leaves

As much as I recommend having citrus around, there are times when I forget to grab lemons and limes on my shop. I keep a stash of fresh lime leaves from my local Asian grocery store in the freezer, and I regularly reach for them to slip into soups, purée into dressings, or simmer in my grains.

### Peas

Fresh peas are one of life's great pleasures. They are tender and sweet and available for only a short few weeks during peak pea season. Outside of pea season, eating a so-called "fresh" pea is like eating a pea-shaped packing peanut and should be avoided at all costs. During those times, frozen peas are still great and are such a handy thing to keep in the freezer, both for the occasional head injury and for getting a quick vegetable on the table.

### Fresh chilies

I buy packs of red Thai chilies, use what I need soon after I bring them home from the grocery store, and freeze the rest to slip whole into curries and soups or to chop and toss into stir-fries and salads. Fresh chilies bring a brightness and even a vegetal quality to dishes that either can stand alone or work with dried chilies and chili flakes for a more complex and nuanced flavour.

### Chicken skins

Waste not, want not. I try to use everything I can from the food I purchase, whether it's cheese rinds, bacon fat, or chicken skin. If I'm cooking chicken in a way that will result in soggy skin, I'll usually remove the skin ahead of time and put it in a small container in the freezer. When I have enough skins, I render them down and use the chicken fat or *schmaltz* (which sounds better, doesn't it?) for roasting vegetables or getting a soup going, and the crispy chicken skin crouton bits for garnishing and adding texture to dishes like Warm Beet Greens in Chicken Skin Vinaigrette (page 78).

# Counter

### Lemons and limes

Nothing brings a big, bold dish to life and makes it sparkle like a squeeze of fresh citrus. I buy both lemons and limes in bulk and use them in just about everything. You can of course keep your citrus in the fridge, but I opt for the counter because I reach for these fruits so often and, candidly, I think they are pretty to look at.

### Unsalted butter

I have listed butter in the counter section because I use room-temperature butter just about every day on toast (page 41), and I like to keep it within easy reach for scrambling eggs or finishing steaks, but I could just as easily have listed it in the fridge and freezer sections because I tend to keep many pounds of butter concurrently: some is stored at room temperature, some is chilled in the fridge, and some is frozen so I never run out.

# Tools and Equipment

This is a list of equipment *suggestions* to make your cooking easier and, in general, your life more enjoyable. I love having beautiful tools and equipment. It feels good to reach for something that is made well and with thought, and to use it for an everyday task like stirring a sauce or rolling out a pie dough. That said, these items do not have to be expensive, and you certainly don't have to run right out and buy them in order to put something delicious on the table.

> It feels good to reach for something that is made well and with thought.

### Sharp chef's knife

A sharp chef's knife is rich advice coming from me since my knife is perpetually dull but, please, get a sharp knife, and take care of it, and it will enhance your cooking experience.

### Paring knife

A little knife that feels good in your hand can be a help and even a joy to use. There's something very satisfying about gripping a paring knife, just so, to peel an apple in one long go or to take the skin off a roasted beet from top to tail in short smooth strips. Have one paring knife that you really like and keep it sharp, as you will reach for it often.

### Serrated knife

A good serrated knife does not have to cost much to do what you need it to do. I cannot even tell you where mine came from, or what brand it is, but it does the job of slicing through crusty bread, separating melon rind from the flesh, and even taking over on slicing tomatoes when my chef's knife gets a bit dull and isn't up to the task.

## Cutting board

Pair your hopefully razor-sharp chef's knife with a sturdy cutting board. I have a huge wooden one that is very thick and doesn't wobble, both of which are qualities you should look for. I use the wrong side for onions and garlic and the right side for vegetables, bread, and pretty much everything else that isn't meat. Owning a smaller plastic cutting board for raw meats and fish that you can fit in the dishwasher is also a big help, but it's not necessary if you are short on space.

## Measuring spoons and cups

A standard set of measuring spoons is a must. While I use my hands (and eyes) frequently to measure things like salt, pepper, and herbs, measuring spoons are non-negotiable for baking and more persnickety recipes. I have a set of Pyrex measuring pitchers for liquid ingredients and a set of metal scoops for dry ingredients. Both sets nest, which saves space. I use them daily for everything from measuring ingredients to make a pot of rice to scooping soup from a pot and transferring it to a zip top bag.

## Mixing bowls

Having a set of metal bowls is just common sense if you plan on mixing things.

## Cast iron skillet

If you can get a cast iron skillet at a thrift store or tag sale, scoop it up, give it a good greasing, and put it to work. A sturdy cast iron pan asks for little in the way of care and will give you so many delicious meals and warm-leftover-pizza-for-breakfast feelings. Because of its thick bottom it will never warp, which enables you to get a good sear on just about anything, and while it's not technically non-stick, a really well-seasoned cast iron skillet will allow you to use less oil than a stainless steel one.

## Medium non-stick skillet

I use my non-stick skillet mostly for eggs and occasionally for a piece of fish.

## Large Dutch oven

This is, hands down, my most used piece of kitchen equipment. I have a chipped, beat-up Le Creuset I bought at Marshalls on sale a decade ago, and I use it every day for cooking, roasting, stewing, and bread baking. Basically, if I'm cooking, it's happening in there. And then! The storage! I love being able to throw the lid back on the pot (upside down usually, since my fridge shelves are close together) and tuck my Dutch oven and its contents back in the fridge for the next day, with the added benefit of being able to reheat everything easily in the same pot.

### Ovenproof baking dishes

A good baking dish is an item that fits neatly into the category of "they just don't make them like they used to." Vintage ovenware pieces have the benefit of being made to last, and they are often very pretty and come with the good feelings of many past delicious meals (and more to come!). Buying them gently used at thrift stores and garage sales makes them more affordable and, for me, a little easier to fill up and give to someone who needs a very large casserole, knowing I might not get it back. I keep something approximating a 9-inch (2.5 L) square baking dish, as well as a 13- × 9-inch (3.5 L) dish and a few miscellaneous sizes in between. Use them for dishes like Tomato Roasted Salmon (page 204), or divide a batch of Sweet Potato Bread Pudding (page 279) into two smaller portions, and bake them in two smaller (but equally beautiful!) vintage baking dishes.

### Three large spatulas (rubber, perforated, and wooden)

I dislike having that one large drawer full of "kitchen utensils" because then I'm always scrabbling around in there looking for the one thing I need, which is not an egg topper or an avocado slicer or a plastic lettuce knife. If I could give a piece of advice: be vigilant about your utensils drawer. The minute people find out you cook, strange unitasking gifts (such as a metal bird that juices lemon wedges) will begin to appear. To avoid clutter or the frustration of being unable to open your drawer because a rogue potato masher has locked it from the inside, you must continually cull the herd, so to speak. There is no recipe I know of that does not require a rubber, a perforated, or a wooden spatula (which is just a wooden spoon with a flat end), so even if you can't bear to part with some of your more superfluous tools, at least keep these on top of everything else.

### Bowl scraper and bench scraper

A bowl scraper is a flexible plastic tool about the size of an index card with a curve on one side. Use it for easing sticky doughs out of bowls, cleaning sticky herbs off your knife, or scraping sticky toddler-craft goo off your counter. A bench scraper has a similar shape but is made of metal and has a wooden or plastic handle. I use mine to transfer chopped things from my cutting board to the bowl or pot it belongs in, for portioning flatbread dough, and for moving ingredients into neat little piles on my cutting board in a very satisfying way.

## Box grater

I like a nice big box grater with a firm handle. Although there are four sides and therefore four grating sizes, I mostly use the largest "setting" for things like making bread crumbs, grating chilled butter for pies, and shredding cheese and veggies.

## Rasp or microplane

There is no better tool for making what my daughters call "snow cheese" than a rasp. It finely grates hard cheese, citrus zest, garlic, spices, you name it. Get a good one, but be careful with it; it will be very sharp, so you must watch your fingers.

## Mandoline

I don't currently own one of these, but I would like to. Mandolines make slicing a breeze, and they allow you to get a uniform thickness, which means everything cooks at the same time or looks fancy. They are extremely sharp, so please use the guard; it's not worth it to be reckless and throw caution to the wind when it comes to your fingertips.

## High-speed blender

A decent-quality high-speed blender is indispensable. It doesn't have to be super-premium like a Blendtec or a Vitamix (although those are nice). For years I used a mid-range Breville, and it definitely got the job done. Use a blender to whizz up a batch of Charred Eggplant Dip (page 33), to blend the silkiest Green Gazpacho with Salmon and Cucumber (page 125), or even to make a delicious Torte in a Hurry (page 273).

## Rolling pin

I like a French rolling pin, which is basically a large wooden dowel that tapers a bit at each end. I am quite short, and for whatever reason I feel I get more leverage with a French rolling pin, but a standard rolling pin works just as well. Make sure it's large and preferably wooden. Use it for rolling out Apple Tart with Rose Cream (page 267) or for smacking your pork chops into an even thickness for Crispy Pork over Many Coloured Tomatoes and Stracciatella (page 228).

## Stand mixer

I resisted having a stand mixer for a long time because, in addition to the expense, I knew it would take up precious counter real estate in my tiny kitchen, but I've found that it makes baking in particular so much easier. Cookies, cakes, breads, whatever—they're all so much easier to knock together if you have a stand mixer.

### Splatter guard

This big, round, metal mesh "lid" lets steam out but keeps liquids (including hot oil) contained. A splatter guard is a must for me, since I have kids constantly underfoot and I want to keep them (and me!) safe. It also makes cleanup easier. If you are simmering or frying, you won't end up with a ring of sauce or grease on your cooking surface.

### Small offset spatula

Cute and useful! Who doesn't like that? Although small, an offset spatula is the perfect thing for swooping frosting, smoothing softened ice cream on a meringue (page 281), flipping a piece of sautéed fish, or even spreading peanut butter on cold chewy toast when "hanger" strikes. They are not expensive, and I guarantee that once you buy one, you'll find yourself reaching for it more than you expect.

### One spoon you love

You should of course have many spoons for eating, unless you live a very spartan existence and keep your cutlery to a minimum, but you should also have one big-ish, feels-right-in-your-hand metal spoon for saucing roasted vegetables, basting meats, dolloping dips, etc. I have a Gray Kunz spoon that goes with me everywhere I cook, and it is endlessly useful.

### Y peeler

If I can avoid peeling vegetables, I do. It's not laziness per se but more about being efficient with my time, as well as embracing the added texture (and nutritional benefits) that come from leaving the skin on. That said, certain things *must* be peeled. Others, like a delicata squash, for example, benefit from a partial peel, where you remove some but not all of the skin in strips. Y peelers—as opposed to a straight swivel peeler—can be used with either hand, allow you to get a good grip, and are the best peeler for the professional and home cook. They are also great for thinly slicing hard cheeses and vegetables and even shaving cold butter for Double Toasted Toaster Toast (page 41).

### Oyster knife

This is not by any means a necessary tool unless you are going to eat oysters at home, which I do recommend (page 21). A sweet little oyster knife with a handle that feels good when you grip it firmly and a sharp point is what you'll need. Oysters (both raw and cooked) are a delicious thing to eat, but you do have to get them open first.

# Breads, Spreads, and More

**Creating an atmosphere of generosity and warmth can be as simple as setting the table.**

When I have people over for dinner, this is usually how the meal goes: I make something bread-y or toast-y, I platter a pile of fresh seafood that hasn't had much done to it, I open a can of stuffed grape leaves and drizzle them in chili oil, I set out a very large piece of cheese that impresses everyone with its sheer magnitude, and I knock together some kind of creamy dip situation. I might toss a simple green salad later in the evening or roast some fish if the oven happens to still be on, but usually any additional dishes feel like overkill because everyone has tucked into so many different flavours already and maybe washed them down with some wine that tastes like beer or beer that tastes like wine.

This chapter is all about easy, choose-your-own-adventure hospitality. You can make a couple of these dishes, such as Oysters and Hot Vinegar (page 21) and Warm Chorizo in Sidra with Charred Bread (page 38), to kick off a meal. You can put out something like the Charred Eggplant Dip (page 33) with a few more substantial dishes from another chapter or some takeout to round out a meal. Or you can make a whole dinner (yes! the whole thing!) by combining several dishes from this chapter, such as Zucchini and Feta Flatbread with Harissa and Pine Nuts (page 49), Butter Beans in Salsa Verde (page 29), and Spicy Marinated Mussels (page 22) with crusty bread and charcuterie.

This is a chapter to begin a meal but also a chapter to begin a book and to ease you into the way I cook and eat. These recipes are meant to be enjoyable for you to prepare. Anything that's a bit fussy (boning the salt cod, kneading flatbread dough) is still fairly mindless and nothing you won't enjoy if you can apply your hands and your mind to a meditative task. Several of the recipes can be made in a matter of minutes, and if you're like me and just a *touch* socially awkward, you can go ahead and keep those in your back pocket for any time you are hosting and need to feel "busy" but not "occupied."

# Oysters and Hot Vinegar

**Serves 4**

3 cups (750 mL) crushed ice

12 oysters

2 tablespoons (30 mL) Hot Vinegar (page 293)

Lemon wedges, to serve

**Tip:** *When shopping for oysters, buy from a local fishmonger if you can. Look for tightly closed oysters that smell like the sea. Once you get the oysters home, give them a scrub under cold running water and store them in the fridge until you're ready to shuck them.*

Oysters are like the little black dress of foods: they go with everything, and you really don't need to do too much to fancy them up. If you want to serve oysters at home—or anywhere—there are really only two things you absolutely have to get right. Make sure your oysters are fresh, and make sure they are served ice cold. If you've never shucked an oyster before, don't worry! It takes a little bit of practice, and maybe a YouTube tutorial or two, but with a positive attitude you can do just about anything.

Fill a large platter with the crushed ice.

Fold a clean kitchen towel in half, top to bottom, and then again, side to side, to create a nice thick rectangle. Place the towel on a sturdy cutting board and set an oyster on top with the tip of the oyster pointing toward your dominant hand. Using your non-dominant hand, fold the towel over the oyster, so that the round end of the oyster is firmly and safely sandwiched between layers of cloth. The point of the oyster should just peek out of the open side of the towel, and your hand should be well away from it, pressing down on the round end of the oyster through the towel.

Using your dominant hand, firmly grip an oyster knife and slip the blade into the space where the shells meet at the point. Wiggle the oyster knife side to side, working your way into the space between the top and bottom shells, while holding all of the things you're supposed to be holding with confidence, until you feel the top part of the oyster start to separate from the bottom. Use the knife to pry the top off the oyster (throw that out) and then slide the knife under the meat of the oyster so that it is still in the shell but not attached to it. Place the oyster, shell side down, gently on the platter of ice. Repeat with the remaining oysters.

Drizzle the oysters with the hot vinegar and serve immediately alongside lemon wedges.

# Spicy Marinated Mussels

### Serves 4 to 6

2 cloves garlic, smashed

2 teaspoons (10 mL) Aleppo pepper

1 teaspoon (5 mL) granulated sugar

3 tablespoons (45 mL) white vinegar

½ cup (125 mL) neutral oil, such as canola or grapeseed

¾ pound (340 g) frozen shelled cooked mussels, thawed and rinsed

Pinch of salt

Juice of ½ lemon

Crusty bread, warm, to serve

This is my take on mussels escabeche, which is a common tinned seafood delicacy in Spain and Portugal. These plump little bivalves are *so good*, especially when they're swimming in spicy oil and vinegar. Served with a hunk of crusty bread, this is my idea of a perfect meal. I always load up on tinned mussels when I find them at specialty shops, but they can be pricey. One day I had a lightbulb moment. I realized I should probably just try making a version at home. These are best if you make them a day or two ahead, so that they really get a chance to marinate and chill, but they are also great served warm on the day you make them.

In a medium saucepan over high heat, whisk together the garlic, Aleppo, sugar, and vinegar. Bring the mixture to a simmer, whisking until the sugar dissolves. Add the oil and whisk to combine. Remove from the heat. Add the mussels and stir to coat them in the liquid. Serve immediately while they are still warm, or store the mussels and liquid in an airtight container in the fridge until ready to serve.

Transfer the mussels and liquid to your preferred serving dish. Season with salt and lemon juice. Serve with warm crusty bread.

Store leftovers in an airtight container in the fridge for up to 3 days.

# Salt Cod Brandade with Herb Salad

**Serves 4 to 6**

### Brandade

1 pound (450 g) salt cod

Small handful of fresh thyme sprigs

1 teaspoon (5 mL) whole black peppercorns

4 cloves garlic, smashed

1 lemon, divided

3 medium russet potatoes

Salt

¼ cup (60 mL) extra-virgin olive oil

½ cup (125 mL) heavy (35%) cream

### Herb Salad

1 cup (250 mL) baby arugula

1 cup (250 mL) fresh flat-leaf parsley

½ cup (125 mL) fresh mint, roughly chopped

¼ cup (60 mL) fresh dill, roughly chopped

2 tablespoons (30 mL) minced chives

1 tablespoon (15 mL) extra-virgin olive oil

1 lemon, juiced

Pinch of ground red chilies

### To serve

1 loaf sourdough bread

1 fennel bulb, sliced

Packages of salt cod are usually found lurking on a fish-adjacent display case in most supermarkets. If you've never opened a packet of salt cod, let me assure you that it is, in fact, exactly what it sounds like. There's even some salt cod out there that has been so salted that it is shelf stable, but the refrigerated version is plenty salty for me, and so that is what I recommend here.

To make the fish edible, you'll need to give it a good soak in cold water overnight—or even for up to a day or two. You don't have to babysit the fish, but if you happen to remember to change the water a few times, it really does help to bring down the saltiness of the fish to a palatable level. There are many different versions of brandade, which is poached salt cod whipped with cream, olive oil, and potatoes, and it can often be quite rich. To temper the richness, I love serving it alongside a fresh herby condiment with bright lemon flavour. I also like serving it with some crisp slices of fennel, which can be used in lieu of bread for schmearing, as a layered item on the bread with the fish and herbs, or simply as a palate cleanser between bites.

**Make the Brandade:** Place the cod in a large airtight container and cover it with cold water. If you have to break up the cod to get it to fit, that's fine. Cover, and place in the fridge to soak overnight or for up to 2 days. If you remember, change the water once or twice. This will help remove as much salt as possible from the fish.

Remove the cod from the water and give it a good rinse under cold running water. One fillet at a time, place it on a cutting board and cut it into chunks about 3 × 6 inches (8 × 15 cm).

Place the cod in a medium saucepan and just cover it with cold water. Add the thyme, peppercorns, and garlic. Slice half of the lemon and add it to the saucepan. Place the saucepan over high heat and bring the water to a boil. Reduce the heat to low and simmer gently until the fish flakes easily with a fork, about 10 to 15 minutes. Remove from the heat and set aside to cool.

*recipe continues*

Peel the potatoes, but don't be fussy about it. Place them in a small saucepan and cover with cold water. Add a generous pinch of salt. Bring to a boil and then reduce the heat to medium and cook until fork tender, about 15 to 20 minutes depending on size. Drain and set aside, but do not allow them to cool completely.

Preheat the oven to 475°F (240°C).

Drain the liquid from the cod and discard the thyme, peppercorns, and garlic. Once the fish is cool enough to handle, use your fingers to remove any skin and bones.

Flake about half of the fish into the bowl of a stand mixer fitted with the paddle attachment. Quarter the hot potatoes and add them to the fish. Mix on low speed for about 1 minute to break up the potatoes. Gradually increase the speed to medium and mix for 1 to 2 minutes. With the mixer running, slowly stream in the olive oil, and then the cream, and continue mixing until all the liquid has been incorporated and the mixture is well combined.

Remove the bowl from the stand mixer. Flake the remaining fish into the bowl and use a rubber spatula to fold it in. You can use the mixer to combine the remaining fish if you want to, but I like to do it by hand so that the mixture remains a bit chunky. Quite a few variables will influence how salty your brandade is at this point, so have a taste and if it needs salt (unlikely!), add more to taste. Squeeze in the juice of the remaining half lemon. Stir to combine.

Transfer the brandade to an 11- × 7-inch (2 L) ovenproof dish. Bake for 7 to 10 minutes, until hot and bubbling. Turn on the broiler and broil for 3 to 5 minutes, until the brandade is golden brown on top. Remove from the oven, and pop the loaf of bread in for 4 to 5 minutes, until charred. Slice the bread.

**Make the Herb Salad:** Wait until the brandade comes out of the oven to make the herb salad, because you want it to be as fresh as possible. In a medium bowl, place the arugula, parsley, mint, dill, and chives. Drizzle the olive oil and lemon juice overtop. Toss to combine. Add the chilies and toss so that all the greens look glossy and fresh.

**To serve:** Set out the brandade, herb salad, hot bread, and fennel slices. Enjoy!

Store leftover brandade in an airtight container in the fridge for up to 3 days. Serve it cold—it will still be perfectly good and schmearable—or reheat it in a small skillet over low heat for a few minutes.

# Butter Beans in Salsa Verde

**Serves 4 to 6**

1 shallot, finely minced

1 teaspoon (5 mL) granulated sugar

2 tablespoons (30 mL) red wine vinegar

1 green chili, minced

1 white anchovy, finely chopped (optional)

½ cup (125 mL) fresh flat-leaf parsley, finely chopped

½ cup (125 mL) fresh cilantro, finely chopped

¾ cup (175 mL) extra-virgin olive oil

1 can (14 ounces/400 mL) butter beans, drained and rinsed

Juice of ½ lemon

Salt and cracked black pepper, to taste

Pinch of ground red chilies

I love big beans and I cannot lie. There's something so meaty and moreish about butter beans, and they look so good on the end of a toothpick that you may feel obligated to serve them when you put out a feast of small dishes for friends. This recipe also fits neatly into the category of "things that happen to be gluten-free and vegan," which can be handy when you're serving a group. The sauce is a simple salsa verde, packed with vinegar, olive oil, tons of herbs, and just a touch of heat, and it's best made fresh so that the herbs don't discolour. The combination of the meaty beans and the bright green sauce hits all the right notes for me. If I'm looking to add a little something extra to this dish to make it a meal, I'll pop a tin of tuna or even cod packed in olive oil into the mix and serve it alongside charred bread.

In a small bowl, whisk together the shallot, sugar, and vinegar until the sugar dissolves. Add the green chili and anchovy (if using). Add the parsley and cilantro. Pour in the olive oil and stir to combine.

Add the beans to the herb mixture. Add the lemon juice and season with salt, pepper, and chilies. Stir to combine and serve immediately.

Store leftovers in an airtight container in the fridge for up to 3 days. The herbs will start to discolour after a day or so, but the dish will still be good to eat.

# Crispy Prosciutto with Melon, Feta, and Mint

**Serves 4 to 6**

4 slices prosciutto

1 small ripe cantaloupe, sliced

1 tablespoon (15 mL) Pickled Chilies (page 291), plus 1 tablespoon (15 mL) brine

1 tablespoon (15 mL) pistachio oil

Juice of 1 lemon

4 ounces (115 g) feta cheese, crumbled, divided

¼ cup (60 mL) toasted pistachios, chopped (see Toasted Nuts, page 290)

Large handful of mint, roughly chopped or torn

Cracked black pepper

Melon and prosciutto are such a classic salty-sweet combo, but here mint, feta, and pistachios add a bit of extra zip and make it less of an antipasto platter and more of a salad. Whenever I eat this dish, I tend to daydream that I'm overlooking the Amalfi Coast with an icy Campari and soda in my hand and an absorbing book on the table next to me. This dream never lasts very long, since my daughters have a way of bursting most of my thought bubbles, but it is a salad we love to share since I am transported and they get excited about eating fruit for dinner.

Preheat the oven to 325°F (160°C). Line a rimmed baking sheet with parchment paper.

Lay out the prosciutto on the prepared baking sheet. Bake for 15 minutes, until crispy. Transfer the prosciutto to a wire rack to cool completely.

Place the cantaloupe, pickled chilies and brine, oil, lemon juice, and about half of the feta in a medium bowl. Toss to combine. Just before serving, crumble in the prosciutto. Add the pistachios, the remaining feta, and the mint. Season with pepper to taste. Serve immediately (with a Campari and soda, if you like).

This salad does not keep particularly well, but if you must, store it in an airtight container in the fridge for up to 1 day.

# Charred Eggplant Dip

**Serves 4 to 6**

1 medium eggplant

1 teaspoon (5 mL) salt, more to taste

1 tablespoon (15 mL) extra-virgin olive oil, more for drizzling

¼ cup (60 mL) tahini

1 tablespoon (15 mL) roughly chopped preserved lemon (optional)

1 tablespoon (15 mL) Garlic Confit (page 286)

¼ cup (60 mL) ice water

½ cup (125 mL) labneh

Juice of ½ lemon

1 teaspoon (5 mL) ground coriander

Flatbread or pita bread, to serve

**Tip:** *If you are pressed for time, you can purchase fire-roasted eggplant in a jar from most Middle Eastern stores. Simply skip the part of the recipe where you roast the eggplant and use about 1½ cups (375 mL) of the prepared eggplant in its place.*

This dip is loosely based on a dish I tried at Andrew Carmellini's restaurant The Dutch more than a decade ago. My friend Hannah Shizgal-Paris worked there for years and generously supplied me with the ingredients list, which I've altered to suit my own pantry and tastes. Stirring labneh into the dip makes it extra creamy, but if you'd like to keep it vegan you can double the amount of tahini and water and the result will still be incredible and more in step with a baba ghanouj.

**Roast the eggplant:** Preheat the oven to 475°F (240°C).

Cut the eggplant in half lengthwise. Using a sharp knife, cut a crosshatch pattern into the cut side of each eggplant, making sure not to poke through the skin. Generously salt the cut sides. Place the eggplant in a colander, cut sides down, and let drain into the sink for about 15 to 20 minutes.

Brush the eggplant flesh with the olive oil and place both halves on a rimmed baking sheet, cut sides down. Roast for 20 minutes, until the skin is slightly charred and the eggplant is tender. Use tongs to return the eggplant to the colander, cut sides down, to cool. Allow any excess juices to drain.

**Make the dip:** In a high-speed blender, pulse the tahini, preserved lemon (if using), and garlic confit until smooth. Scoop the eggplant flesh out of its skin. Discard the skin. Add half of the eggplant flesh to the blender and pulse again two or three times to briefly combine. With the blender running on high speed, slowly stream in the water. Continue blending until the mixture becomes smooth, pale, and thick.

Transfer the contents of the blender to a small bowl. Add the remaining eggplant flesh and the labneh and stir to combine. Add more salt to taste. If serving immediately, drizzle with additional olive oil and the lemon juice. Sprinkle the coriander on top. Serve with warm flatbread, pita bread, or other dunkable things.

Store the dip, ungarnished and covered, in the refrigerator for up to 3 days. Give it a brief stir before serving.

# Creamy Radish Dip

## Serves 4 to 6

### Dip

¼ cup (60 mL) unsalted butter, softened

6 ounces (170 g) full-fat plain cream cheese, softened

1 tablespoon (15 mL) brine from Pickled Chilies (page 291)

Dash of Worcestershire sauce

¼ cup (60 mL) sliced scallions

1 cup (250 mL) chopped radishes

2 tablespoons (30 mL) Pickled Chilies (page 291), finely chopped

### To serve

Handful of celery leaves, roughly chopped

3 to 4 radishes, thinly sliced

Pinch of ground red chilies

1 bunch celery, cut into sticks

Ritz crackers

When I was growing up, my mom always made this radish dip for cocktail hour on special occasions. She would mix all the grown-ups a drink and put out little dishes of homemade Bits n' Bites, crackers, and this dip, which always feels festive to me because of the red radishes. The dip was delicious and never lasted very long, especially if my brothers got to it first. I've made a few small updates to the ingredients list (namely, I've added a splash of brine from my Pickled Chilies, page 291) but left the spirit of the recipe intact with all its radish-y, creamy, crunchy, hint-of-nostalgia goodness. If you don't have the Pickled Chiles on hand, they take about an hour to prepare and pickle before you start this recipe; or you can use about 1 teaspoon (5 mL) white vinegar, a pinch of sugar, and a few pinches of ground red chilies to make a reasonable facsimile.

**Make the Dip:** In the bowl of a stand mixer fitted with the paddle attachment, combine the butter, cream cheese, brine, and Worcestershire sauce on medium speed for 2 to 3 minutes, until smooth. Remove the bowl from the stand mixer and, using a rubber spatula, fold in the scallions, chopped radishes, and pickled chilies, until just combined.

**To serve:** Transfer the dip to a serving dish. Garnish with the celery leaves, sliced radish, and chilies. Serve immediately alongside celery sticks and Ritz crackers.

Leftover dip can be stored in an airtight container in the fridge for up to 2 days, but the radishes will lose their crunch. This dish is best served fresh.

# Baked Red Pepper Butter with Goat Cheese

## Serves 4 to 6

6 medium red bell peppers, seeded, ribs removed, and roughly chopped

3 cloves Garlic Confit (page 286)

Pinch of ground red chilies

Pinch of salt

¼ cup (60 mL) extra-virgin olive oil, more for drizzling

1 cup (250 mL) water

1 tablespoon (15 mL) white vinegar or Hot Vinegar (page 293)

1 teaspoon (5 mL) granulated sugar

4 ounces (115 g) goat cheese

Flakey salt

Charred bread, to serve

Look, I get it. Goat cheese isn't that cool anymore. It had a moment, and most of us were there for it. It was right around the time people were giving out bottles of balsamic reduction as hostess gifts, sundried tomatoes suddenly appeared on pizza, and comically large pepper grinders emerged every time you ordered a garden salad. But not for nothing is goat cheese still around. It's not cool, but it is—and I'm being objective here, I promise—*good*. It has the tart, brined taste of feta but without the more granular mouthfeel. Here, goat cheese is paired with slow-cooked red peppers swimming in a bit of extra-virgin olive oil, then sent for a ride in the oven to get hot and bubbly and very schmearable.

Preheat the oven to 475°F (240°C).

Place the peppers in a medium skillet with the garlic confit, chilies, and pinch of salt. Drizzle with the olive oil. Cover and cook over medium heat for 20 minutes, stirring occasionally. Increase the heat to high and add the water, stirring so that the mixture does not burn. Continue to cook for 5 to 10 minutes, until the water is reduced and the peppers become very soft. Use a spoon to break up the peppers a bit. Stir in the vinegar and sugar and cook for 1 minute more.

Transfer the mixture to a small skillet or ovenproof dish that can hold about 4 cups (1 L). Crumble or smash the goat cheese evenly on top. Bake for 5 to 7 minutes, until bubbling.

Carefully remove the pepper butter from the oven. Give it a quick stir. Drizzle with olive oil and a sprinkle of flakey salt. Serve with charred bread.

Store leftovers in an airtight container in the fridge for up to 5 days. Warm or cold, leftover pepper butter makes an excellent spread for all manner of sandwiches and sandwich-like foods.

# Warm Chorizo in Sidra with Charred Bread

**Serves 4 to 6**

8 ounces (225 g) Spanish chorizo, sliced into ½-inch (1 cm) rounds

2 cups (500 mL) Spanish sidra or dry apple cider

Charred bread, to serve

I really can't do justice to this dish by describing it because it is, in essence, just hot sausage floating in warm fermented apple juice, which might not make you feel compelled to make it. But you're just going to have to trust me that a sort of alchemy takes place during cooking. The sausage gets a little soft and sweet, and the sidra, which is just a very dry Spanish apple cider with a low alcohol by volume, gets spicy and a little smoky and becomes more than the sum of its parts. Find sidra at most specialty wine shops or substitute a dry apple cider or even a dry white wine for a similar effect. Spooning some of this brothy chorizo onto a charred piece of bread (by candlelight, if possible) is one of life's great simple pleasures and feels somehow both glamourous and cozy.

Place the chorizo in a small saucepan and cover with the sidra. Bring to a boil over high heat. Reduce the heat to low and let simmer gently for 8 to 10 minutes until the chorizo is warmed through and its flavour has infused the sidra. Serve immediately alongside charred bread for dipping.

Store leftovers in an airtight container in the fridge for up to 4 days. Warm gently in a saucepan before serving.

# Toast under Everything

Many of the recipes in this book call for charred bread. And really, that's just a fancy way of saying "toast."

Toast is one of those foods I have a practical attachment to because it simplifies the task of making a quick dinner. You can slather it with Feta Cream (page 294) and drizzle it with some Hot Honey (page 293), you can nestle it next to a bowl of Lentil Soup (page 130) or Corn, Bacon, and Mussel Chowder (page 192) to complete a meal, or it can help make leftovers seem special—a piece of Olive Oil Fried Bread (page 42) slathered with Tahini Dip (page 294) and topped with a few slices of cold Prosciutto Wrapped Eggplant (page 142) and a fistful of arugula is truly so delicious.

But toast is also a food that feeds my heart. One of my first food memories is of eating toast at our babysitter's house. Dorinda was a cozy woman with the kind of lap you could sink into for hours and arms big and strong enough to wrap around two toddlers at the same time. My older brother, Geoffrey, and I were devoted to her. Each afternoon, at more or less the same time, she made a very large production of making herself toast. She would place white bread from the grocery store in the toaster and plunge the lever down with a metallic click. Once the bread reemerged with a bit of a tan, she would place it on a china plate and briskly spread margarine over it. The sound of the knife scraping against the toast was the cue for my brother and I to hide behind a large, overstuffed chair in the living room. Dorinda would then carry the plate of toast into the room where we were hiding very poorly and loudly, set it down, and then announce to no one in particular, "Oh, I've forgotten to get my tea." As soon as she left the room, my brother and I would tumble out from behind the chair, eat the toast with crumbs flying everywhere, and then return to our hiding place where we would wait for Dorinda to realize we had tricked her *again*. We repeated this ritual every day until our family moved to another town. It's probably the reason that I love dinner theatre and that a cold, chewy piece of toasted Wonder Bread with margarine is, to me, still a very delicious thing to eat.

If you are not yet a toast aficionado, here are a few ways I like to experience it.

**Olive Oil Fried Bread**

Get one or two good, thick slices of sourdough bread. You want the bread to have some air bubbles in the crumb so that it fries nicely, but not so many that it is not structurally sound for all the toppings you will no doubt pile on it shortly. Line a large plate with paper towels.

In a large cast iron skillet, heat about 2 tablespoons (30 mL) of olive oil—or enough to cover the bottom of your skillet—over high heat. Once the oil starts to shimmer, add the bread, using either tongs or a perforated spatula to press it gently into the oil. Keep the heat on high for about 1 minute until the bread starts to visibly brown, then reduce the heat to medium and fry for another 2 to 3 minutes, until golden brown. Increase the heat to high and flip the bread over, frying it in the same manner as you fried the first side. Once the bread is golden brown and crispy all over, transfer it to the prepared plate. Sprinkle with a bit of flakey salt, if desired. Load up the fried bread with toppings and eat.

**Grilled Bread**

Preheat a grill or grill pan to 500°F (260°C), or until it is very hot. Get one or two slices of sourdough, multigrain, or rye bread. Brush both sides of the bread with olive oil, then sprinkle with a bit of kosher salt.

Lay the bread diagonally on the grill or grill pan (the diagonal placement is not strictly a technique; I just like the way the grill marks look) and let the bread grill for 2 to 3 minutes, undisturbed, until it has clear grill marks. Flip the bread and repeat. Once the bread is charred evenly on both sides, transfer it to a platter, perhaps alongside some Butter Beans in Salsa Verde (page 29) or Warm Chorizo in Sidra (page 38) and enjoy.

**Double Toasted Toaster Toast**

The homiest of toasts! This is the toast I make on cold mornings, on rushed evenings after work when I have all kinds of "hangry" feelings, or even when I just need a bit of comfort. For this toast, a good slice of basic white or brown bread is my favourite.

Simply put the bread in the toaster on the maximum setting and push the lever. When the toast pops, repeat the process. Double Toasted Toaster Toast is best eaten after it has cooled slightly.

On days when I really feel a need, I like to spread a thin layer of room-temperature butter on the bread, let it stand for 1 or 2 minutes to melt, and then shave cold butter from the fridge on top of the other butter, followed by a drizzle of Hot Honey (page 293) and a sprinkling of flakey salt. This is very good and very restorative, especially when paired with hot tea and a book that doesn't require much in the way of effort to read.

# Baked Cheese with Hot Honey

**Serves 4 to 6**

8 ounces (225 grams) époisses, camembert, or brie cheese

1 clove garlic

2 tablespoons (30 mL) dry white wine

2 tablespoons (30 mL) Hot Honey (page 293)

Charred bread and/or crackers, to serve

This recipe for baked cheese is so simple and so perfect. There is nothing extra here; you will find only hot, oozy—and just a touch boozy—cheese. In a nod to the 1970s-era kitsch within which this dish was likely conceived, I like to serve it in the little wooden box the cheese comes in. I recommend époisses cheese here, which you can find at most specialty cheese shops, but a decent-quality camembert or brie will be fine as well. Baked cheese is not here to be fancy, but it will steal the show, and it will, without a doubt, be replicated by all your friends in due course because, honestly, what's not to love?

Preheat the oven to 425°F (220°C).

Remove the cheese from its round wooden box. Wrap the entire box in aluminum foil. Return the cheese to the foil-wrapped box and place it on a rimmed baking sheet.

Using a paring knife, poke a small hole in the top of the cheese and push in the garlic clove. Drizzle the wine into the hole and over the top of the cheese. Bake for 15 to 20 minutes, until hot and bubbly.

Drizzle the cheese with the hot honey and serve immediately with charred bread and/or crackers.

It's unlikely you will have any leftovers—we're talking hot cheese here, after all—but you can store any remaining cheese in an airtight container in the fridge for up to 4 days

# Garlic Fingers

## Serves 4 to 6

**Béchamel Sauce**

1¼ cups (300 mL) whole milk (3.25%)
   or 2% milk

3 white anchovies, plus 1 teaspoon
   (5 mL) of their oil

2 cloves garlic

2 tablespoons (30 mL) unsalted butter

2 tablespoons (30 mL) all-purpose flour

Salt and cracked black pepper

**Garlic Fingers**

½ batch Flatbread Dough (page 298)

1 clove garlic

1 cup (250 mL) shredded mozzarella

Small handful of fresh flat-leaf parsley,
   chopped

Where I am from, on the east coast of Canada, garlic fingers are a *thing*. Not quite a pizza, and not really a breadstick—or even a finger, come to think of it. Affectionately known as "garlies," they hang out in that delicious yet excessive category of "party food," which also tends to include foods one might want to eat quite late on a cold Halifax night while staggering down Barrington Street looking for enough sustenance to make it all the way home. Although white anchovies are not a typical ingredient, I like the extra-briny ocean flavour they add because it makes the garlic fingers taste even more like home.

**Make the Béchamel Sauce:** In a small saucepan over high heat, bring the milk, anchovies plus their oil, and garlic to a boil. Reduce the heat to medium and let simmer for 1 minute. Turn off the heat, cover, and let steep for about 10 minutes. Fish out the garlic and discard.

In a medium saucepan over medium heat, melt the butter. Sprinkle in the flour. Whisk the mixture continuously, so it does not scorch or stick to the pan, for about 2 to 3 minutes until a thick paste forms. Whisk in the hot milk mixture. Continue cooking for another 5 minutes to make a thick sauce. Season with salt and pepper to taste.

**Make the Garlic Fingers:** Preheat the oven to 500°F (260°C). Lightly grease a large baking sheet with olive oil.

Roll out the dough into a large rectangle a little bit smaller than the baking sheet. Transfer it to the baking sheet. Dollop the béchamel sauce on top.

Using a rasp, grate the garlic over the béchamel. Sprinkle the mozzarella evenly overtop. Bake for 8 to 10 minutes, or until the dough is golden brown and the cheese is melted and bubbling. Remove the baking sheet from the oven and sprinkle the parsley evenly overtop the flatbread. Return to the oven for another 2 minutes. Immediately transfer the flatbread to a wire rack and let cool for 5 to 10 minutes. Slice the bread into "fingers" and serve warm.

Store leftovers in an airtight container in the fridge for up to 5 days.

# Zucchini and Feta Flatbread with Harissa and Pine Nuts

**Serves 4 to 6**

1 batch Flatbread Dough (page 298)

½ cup (125 mL) Harissa (page 296), more for drizzling

1 small green zucchini, thinly sliced

4 ounces (115 g) Macedonian feta

1 cup (250 mL) baby arugula

2 tablespoons (30 mL) toasted pine nuts (see Toasted Nuts, page 290)

As a kid, I really did not enjoy soft foods. My parents tried with great enthusiasm to get me to like zucchini, but because they consistently overcooked it, I simply could not get on board despite their multiple attempts—even an effort to rebrand it when they presented it as "courgette." It wasn't until I tried zucchini again as an adult, in preparations where it was just barely cooked or even raw, that I found I actually loved zucchini. Here, it is thinly sliced and not cooked much at all. I love the way it still holds a bit of its structure, but also softens just a little without losing its subtle flavour. It's paired with a homemade Harissa (page 296), creamy Macedonian feta, peppery arugula, and a few toasty pine nuts on a giant flatbread. What a great way to enjoy this amazing vegetable. Even if you are zucchini-averse, this dish might just change your mind!

Preheat the oven to 425°F (220°C). Grease a baking sheet with olive oil.

Roll out the dough into a rectangle about the size of the baking sheet. Carefully transfer the dough to the prepared baking sheet.

Gently spread the harissa over the dough in an even layer. Arrange the zucchini on top.

Bake for 12 to 14 minutes, until the crust is golden brown. Remove the flatbread from the oven and crumble the feta evenly on top. Return to the oven just long enough for the cheese to soften a bit, 1 minute tops.

Garnish the flatbread with the arugula and pine nuts. Drizzle with a bit more harissa. Serve warm if desired, but this is also excellent served cold or at room temperature.

Store leftovers in an airtight container in the fridge for up to 5 days.

# A Side of Vegetables

**The longer I want a dinner to last, the more vegetables I serve.**

I don't mean volume necessarily (although I do love the look of abundance), but I do serve a variety of vegetables. I like to think about the way vegetable dishes will play off each other: What will be the spicy dish? The crunchy one? Which platter will I turn to when I want to cool my mouth? Is something eye-wateringly acidic? (I hope so!) What's raw? What is cooked? If there's a little bit of everything, I can move around my plate and find tastes that are both familiar and surprising. I can take my time and enjoy not just what is in front of me but also the people around me.

Because vegetable sides are a bit smaller and not necessarily meant to be the focus of a meal, I also find you can really swing for the fences in terms of flavour profile or even, as is the case with something like a Tartiflette (page 102) or a Butternut Squash and Sharp Cheddar Gratin (page 101), go all-in on a vegetable dish that is as rich as it is delicious.

Of course, in this section you'll find sturdy salads, such as Every Night Salad (page 53), and old favourites that have been thoughtfully reimagined, such as Braised Red Cabbage with Cider and Bacon (page 85), but there are also things to liven up your vegetable party that you may not have tried before. Lemony Spaghetti Squash with Burrata and Herbs (page 68) and Warm Beet Greens in Chicken Skin Vinaigrette (page 78) are dishes that really celebrate what it is to love vegetables. These are dishes that I believe have the potential to become a talking point or, even better, if they are really well received, the kind of dishes that are relished in thoughtful silence.

# Every Night Salad

**Serves 4**

½ small white onion, thinly sliced

½ head of iceberg lettuce, chopped

½ seedless cucumber, chopped

2 vine-ripened tomatoes, chopped

1 cup (250 mL) loosely packed soft herbs, such as mint, dill, and parsley, roughly chopped

Salt and cracked black pepper

1 tablespoon (15 mL) Tartar Sauce (page 295)

2 tablespoons (30 mL) white vinegar

Small handful of edible flowers, such as nasturtiums or pansies (optional)

**Tip:** *Allowing raw onions to sit in cold water for even a few minutes will help remove some of their sting.*

Iceberg lettuce is my favourite of all the lettuces, and I feel strongly that it doesn't get as much respect as it deserves. Ditto white vinegar, which has all the sharp, mouthwatering acidity I'm looking for in an everyday vinegar, plus a clean and neutral flavour. In this salad, I combine both of these with the freshest herbs I can find, some basic produce staples, and just a smidge of tartar sauce, which gives all that good crunchy stuff a hint of creamy-pickle magic. Edible flowers, which may seem like a chef's touch, are simply a nod to my daughters. We plant nasturtiums every spring, and adding a handful of these pretty petals is the kind of joyful touch that brings a little brightness to any dinner, no matter how old or young you may be.

Place the onions in a small bowl of ice water and let stand for about 5 minutes.

In a large salad bowl, place the lettuce, cucumber, tomatoes, and herbs. Season with salt and pepper to taste. Gently toss to combine.

In a small bowl, whisk together the tartar sauce and vinegar. Remove the onions from the ice water and add them to the salad along with the dressing. Gently toss the salad again, until the lettuce is evenly coated with dressing. Season with more pepper to taste. Garnish with edible flowers (if using). Serve immediately.

# Italian Chop

**Serves 4 to 6**

1 small bulb of fennel, thinly sliced

1 small head of radicchio, thinly sliced

1 small head of Belgian endive, thinly sliced

½ cup (125 mL) toasted hazelnuts, chopped (see Toasted Nuts, page 290)

2 cups (500 mL) baby arugula

Zest and juice of 1 lemon

2 tablespoons (30 mL) hazelnut oil, more for drizzling

1 cup (250 mL) grated pecorino cheese

Salt and cracked black pepper, to taste

I love a salad where everything is just *heaped* together and really jumbled so that every bite has a bit of this and a bit of that. A proper tossed salad is a beautiful thing, and this one has all the flavours I want. Thinly sliced fennel adds both sweetness and crunch, while radicchio and endive lettuces both contribute fresh and bitter elements. Arugula brings a peppery note, and the hazelnuts and pecorino cheese keep all the ingredients in balance with their nutty flavours. When you tumble everything together with lots of acidic lemon, the effect is super delicious and a pleasure to eat.

Place all ingredients in a large bowl and toss very well to combine. Pour a final drizzle of hazelnut oil on top. Serve immediately.

Store leftovers in an airtight container in the fridge for up to 3 days. I wouldn't recommend serving leftovers again on their own, but they do taste good stuffed into a sandwich with prosciutto or some roasted eggplant.

# Caesar Beans

## Serves 4

1 pound (450 g) haricots verts

2 cloves Garlic Confit (page 286)

Juice of 1 lemon

1 egg yolk

2 teaspoons (10 mL) capers

½ teaspoon (2 mL) Worcestershire sauce

½ teaspoon (2 mL) fish sauce

¼ cup (60 mL) finely grated Parmesan
cheese

½ cup extra-virgin olive oil

Cracked black pepper

### To garnish

4 to 5 white anchovies

¼ cup (60 mL) finely grated Parmesan
cheese

¼ cup (60 mL) Bread Crumbs (page 289)

2 tablespoons (30 mL) Crispy Shallots
(page 287)

The part of eating a Caesar salad I like the most is when I get a big, crunchy romaine rib smothered in lemony-fishy dressing, a reasonable amount of black pepper, and definitely a borderline-unreasonable amount of Parmesan cheese. Blanched haricots verts (which are like a green bean but skinnier) have an intense snappiness, with the added bonus of delicious green bean flavour. Cover the beans in just enough crunchy garnishes, snowy cheese, and glittering little fish to make it look super elegant and—voilà!—a dish that that may just replace the original in my recipe roster.

Bring a large saucepan of salted water to a boil. Fill a medium bowl halfway with water and ice.

Drop the haricots verts into the boiling water, and give them a quick stir to make sure they are all submerged. Cook for about 1 minute. Once they turn a vibrant green colour, cook for an additional 1 minute. Using tongs, transfer the beans to the prepared bowl of ice water to cool. This will stop the cooking so that they remain tender but crisp.

Place the garlic confit, lemon juice, egg yolk, capers, Worcestershire sauce, fish sauce, and Parmesan in a high-speed blender. Pulse to combine. With the blender on low speed, slowly stream in the olive oil, blending until fully incorporated. Check the seasoning and, if desired, add pepper to taste. Blend for a few more seconds to combine.

Drain the haricots verts and pat them dry with a clean kitchen towel. Transfer the beans to a medium bowl or platter. Pour the dressing overtop. Toss until evenly coated. Top with a few more grinds of pepper, the anchovies, Parmesan, bread crumbs, and crispy shallots. Serve immediately.

Store leftovers in an airtight container in the fridge for up to 2 days. The beans may get a bit soggy, but they will still be good to eat.

# Raw Corn and Feta Salad

**Serves 4**

½ cup (125 mL) Feta Cream (page 294)

6 ears of corn, kernels removed and cobs discarded

4 ounces (115 g) feta, plus 1 tablespoon (15 mL) brine

3 radishes, thinly sliced

2 scallions, thinly sliced

Zest and juice of 2 limes

2 tablespoons (30 mL) extra-virgin olive oil

Pinch of ground red chilies

Salt, to taste

1 cup (250 mL) loosely packed fresh basil, roughly chopped or torn

Chili oil or Chili Crisp (page 288), for drizzling

In peak season, at the height of summer, raw corn is a treat. It's sweeter and juicier at this time of year and has plenty of crunch. You can eat it right off the cob, maybe with a drizzle of lime, and be totally happy. You can also, as I do here, take those two ingredients—fresh corn and lime—and add *mounds* of feta, a few radishes, scallions, and herbs for a salad that is fresh and fast. As a lazy summer day bonus, it also will not require you to cook anything.

Schmear a large plate or platter with the feta cream. In a medium bowl, place the corn, feta, radishes, scallions, lime zest and juice, olive oil, chilies, and salt. Toss thoroughly to combine.

Heap the corn mixture onto the feta cream. Top with the basil and a drizzle of chili oil. Serve immediately.

Store leftovers in an airtight container in the fridge for up to 4 days.

# Cucumbers with Chili and Scallions

**Serves 4**

6 Persian cucumbers

Pinch of kosher salt

3 tablespoons (45 mL) Chili Crisp (page 288)

Sesame oil, for drizzling

1 tablespoon (15 mL) toasted sesame seeds

2 scallions, ends trimmed and thinly sliced

The first time I had Szechuan food, I can't actually tell you where I was. I remember clambering into the back of a car (or was it a van?) with the kitchen crew from Mile End Deli in Brooklyn. They took me on a winding, fast-paced drive to an incredible restaurant that changed the way I thought about food forever. I'd had spicy food before, and I'd had Chinese food before in various combinations, but the flavour of Szechuan food specifically—and the numbing effect that Szechuan peppercorns have—was new to me. There's something hard to pin down about the flavour of Szechuan peppercorns. They have an almost piney quality that makes them complex as well as, well, spicy.

This recipe, which is simple to prepare and found at most Szechuan restaurants, can be made with homemade Chili Crisp (page 288) or any number of store-bought versions (see page 288 for recommendations). It can be served alongside just about anything from Flank Steak with Salsa Verde and Cumin Smashed Potatoes (page 239) to Herb Stuffed Rainbow Trout (page 200), as well as stuffed into a sandwich or simply spooned over rice.

Lay a cucumber horizontally in front of you on a sturdy wooden cutting board. Trim off the ends. With confidence and a rolling pin, smack the cucumber two or three times so that it breaks up a bit. Place it in a medium bowl and repeat with the remaining cucumbers.

Using your hands, tear the cucumbers into large bite-size pieces. Sprinkle with the salt and let stand for 10 minutes. This will help remove some of the excess water from the cucumbers and temper the grassy flavour. Drain any liquid in the bowl. Add the chili crisp and toss to combine. Drizzle with the sesame oil, and sprinkle the sesame seeds and scallions on top. Toss a final time and serve immediately.

Store leftovers in an airtight container in the fridge for up to 3 days. The cucumbers will lose some of their crunch, but they will still be good to eat.

# Celery with Walnuts, Feta, and Dill

**Serves 4**

1 bunch of celery, thinly sliced

4 ounces (115 g) feta, crumbled, plus 1 tablespoon (15 mL) brine

Juice of 1 lemon

½ cup (125 mL) walnuts, toasted and roughly chopped (see Toasted Nuts, page 290)

½ cup (125 mL) fresh dill, chopped

¼ cup (60 mL) walnut oil, more for drizzling

Pinch of ground red chilies

Celery often plays a supporting role to other vegetables despite the fact that it has many wonderful characteristics, including a subtle but totally unique flavour, miraculous refrigerator longevity, and a high water content that ensures crisp, fresh flavour in any dish where it appears.

In this salad, celery is combined with just a handful of simple ingredients. The sweetness of the dill paired with the salty feta and toasted nuts allows the celery to really *be the celery* in a meaningful way. This is such a simple dish to make, and it is versatile too. Pair it with Harissa Chicken (page 213) and some warm pita and Charred Eggplant Dip (page 33) or serve it next to Pan Seared Ribeyes with Ramp and Anchovy Butter (page 241) for a complete meal.

Place the celery, feta, lemon juice, walnuts, dill, walnut oil, and chilies in a medium bowl. Toss to combine. Pour a final drizzle of walnut oil over the salad. Serve immediately.

Store leftovers in an airtight container in the fridge for up to 2 days. The celery may lose some of its crunch, but it will still be good to eat.

# Garlicky Greens with Soy Sauce

**Serves 4**

1 small head of broccoli, woody ends trimmed

1 bunch broccoli rabe, woody ends trimmed

6 heads of baby bok choy

2 tablespoons (30 mL) neutral oil, such as canola or grapeseed

2 cloves garlic, smashed

½ cup (125 mL) chicken stock

1 tablespoon (15 mL) soy sauce

1 tablespoon (15 mL) oyster sauce

2 teaspoons (10 mL) sesame oil

1 green chili, thinly sliced

This is one of those dishes that I'd like to be eating 5 minutes after the thought of it pops into my head. It is a riff on the Chinese broccoli smothered in oyster sauce that you often see at dim sum restaurants, which is a thing I always *have* to order. I love the bright green crispness, and I love it even more covered in a garlicky, funky, umami sauce. At home, I like to use a mix of whatever green vegetables I have on hand. The addition of green chili is not traditional, but I like the pops of spice it adds.

Use a vegetable peeler to peel the tough outer skin from the broccoli stem. Using a sharp knife, divide the broccoli into about 6 or 8 pieces, leaving the stems attached. Place the broccoli in a medium bowl and set aside.

Using your knife, chop the leafy tops from the broccoli rabe. Place the stems in the bowl with the broccoli. Place the leafy tops in a small bowl. Set aside.

Cut the bok choy in half lengthwise and trim out the core, leaving a small amount so that the leaves remain attached. Place the bok choy in the bowl with the broccoli and broccoli rabe stems.

In a large saucepan with a lid, cook the oil and garlic over medium-high heat until the oil starts to shimmer and the garlic starts to turn golden. Add the broccoli, broccoli rabe stems, and bok choy. Increase the heat to high and stir the vegetables so that they do not burn. Cook for 1 to 2 minutes, until the vegetables are bright green. Carefully pour in the chicken stock and cover immediately. Cook for about 2 minutes, until the vegetables are tender. Turn off the heat. Add the leafy tops of the broccoli rabe and put the lid back on. Let stand for 1 to 2 minutes, until the leafy tops are wilted. Stir to ensure that they are fully wilted.

Drizzle the soy sauce, oyster sauce, and sesame oil over the vegetables. Toss to coat evenly. Top with the green chili. Serve immediately.

Store leftovers in an airtight container in the fridge for up to 5 days.

# The Way My Mother Cooked

My mother cooked us dinner every night. And I do mean *cooked*. Of course, there was the occasional President's Choice "Memories of Saigon" Peanut Butter Pad Thai, or a couple of pizzas from that place in the supermarket plaza that had the best coupons, but in general my mother sliced, grated, chopped, and stirred her way through recipe cards or newspaper clippings on most evenings. Until I had my own children, I didn't understand that the effort she put into this part of our lives was exceptional. Not just in terms of the food she prepared, but in the variety.

When I think of the food of my childhood, there is no one iconic dish that transports me to our family table. There is only a feeling. The feeling is of my mother standing by the sink, wearing a green Pete's Frootique apron and perhaps a semi-charred oven mitt. There were always pots on the stove and things in the oven, a glass of scotch or red wine on the counter, and CBC's *As It Happens* burbling in the background.

A prairie girl, my mother did not adhere to a specific style of cooking, so it was all on the table, so to speak. She'd plan to get the right ingredients on her Sunday shop, or even visit a specialty store for the perfect sherry vinegar or real corn tortillas, and then take a shot at any recipe that piqued her interest. One night, it might be a South African meat pie from *The Chez Piggy Cookbook*, another evening a layered ham salad from *Chatelaine* served in a giant glass trifle dish. There were gazpacho, cabbage rolls, red pepper chicken, quiche—the list goes on and on to as many recipes as she could snip out of the paper or dog-ear in her cookbooks.

And what a wonderful thing that was. To have a mother who was interested in food and in making it for three children who probably would have happily lived on cold Hot Pockets, had they been permitted to do so.

It was not until much later that I realized how far above and beyond she went, not just in her cooking but in the confidence with which she tackled new flavours and techniques. Things don't always work out, in recipes or in life, but the thing I learned from watching my mother was that you can always choose to believe they will and swing for the fences. Sometimes, you hit a home run. Sometimes, you fail. But you can always order pizza.

# Lemony Spaghetti Squash with Burrata and Herbs

**Serves 4**

1 medium spaghetti squash, halved and seeded

1 clove garlic, smashed

2 teaspoons (10 mL) + 2 tablespoons (30 mL) extra-virgin olive oil, divided

1 teaspoon (5 mL) salt, more to taste

Juice of 1 lemon

Pinch of ground red chilies

Cracked black pepper

1 cup (250 mL) loosely packed soft herbs such as basil, mint, and parsley

8 ounces (225 g) burrata cheese

Chili oil, for drizzling

Squash is often overlooked in the summer months, even though it grows terrifically well alongside the tomatoes, peppers, and zucchini most people associate with a summer garden. I like this dish because it shows how bright and versatile squash is, but also because you can put it together in a lazy summer way where you roast the squash and then let it hang out for a bit while you get the other ingredients ready, water the aforementioned tomatoes, peppers, and zucchini, or enjoy a quiet glass of piquette. Serving the squash at room temperature may be surprising, but once you dig in to it with the burrata, lemon, and herbs, it will all make sense and you will want to do it again and again.

Preheat the oven to 425°F (220°C). Line a rimmed baking sheet with parchment paper or foil.

Rub the cut sides of the squash with the garlic. Drizzle the inside of each squash half with about 1 teaspoon (5 mL) olive oil. Sprinkle with the salt and place the squash, cut side down, on the prepared baking sheet.

Roast for 30 to 40 minutes, or until the squash is tender and easily pulls away from the skin with a fork. Flip the squash halves so that they are cut side up. Let cool to room temperature.

Using a fork, scrape the squash flesh into strands. Transfer the flesh to a medium bowl. Toss the squash with the remaining 2 tablespoons (30 mL) olive oil, the lemon juice, and chilies. Season with the salt and pepper to taste. Fold in about half of the herbs. Place the squash on a large platter. Working over the squash to catch any drips, tear the burrata into 2 or 3 chunks and garnish with the remaining herbs. Drizzle with the chili oil. Serve immediately.

Store leftovers in an airtight container in the fridge for up to 3 days.

# Leeks in Vinaigrette with Black Olives and Bread Crumbs

## Serves 4 to 6

2 bunches leeks

4 ounces (115 g) goat cheese, room temperature

2 tablespoons (30 mL) extra-virgin olive oil, more to taste

Juice of 1 lemon

¼ cup (60 mL) fresh tarragon, roughly chopped

½ cup (125 mL) black olives, pitted

½ cup (125 mL) Bread Crumbs (page 289)

For me, having a small and not terribly prolific garden is mostly about having an activity to do with my daughters, or even a place to go and putter when I need a break from the indoors. But it's also made me think about the vegetables I see at the grocery store in a different way. Even if I can't grow everything on my grocery list, I'm better at knowing exactly what is in season when. Leeks start to pop up in the early summer, and this dish is the perfect thing to make at that time. It's bright and casually elegant and looks as comfortable next to Pan Seared Ribeyes with Ramp and Anchovy Butter (page 241) as it does next to a platter of Prosciutto Wrapped Eggplant (page 142).

Bring a large saucepan of salted water to a boil. While you're waiting for the water to boil, fill a medium bowl halfway with water and ice.

Trim the dark green parts from the leeks and discard, or save for future use in a stock or soup. Drop the leeks into the boiling water and blanch for 4 to 5 minutes, until they are easily pierced with a paring knife. Immediately plunge the leeks into the prepared bowl of ice water and let cool completely. Drain and pat dry. Slice the leeks into 1-inch (2.5 cm) rounds.

Schmear a large plate or platter with the goat cheese. Arrange the leeks on top. Drizzle the olive oil and lemon juice overtop. Sprinkle with the tarragon, olives, and bread crumbs and drizzle with additional olive oil, if desired.

Store leftovers in an airtight container in the fridge for up to 5 days.

# Pan Fried Brussels Sprouts with Lemon and Pecorino

**Serves 4**

¼ cup (60 mL) neutral oil, such as grapeseed or canola

1½ pounds (675 g) Brussels sprouts, thinly sliced

½ teaspoon (2 mL) salt

1 teaspoon (5 mL) Dijon mustard

Pinch of dried red chilies

Juice of ½ lemon

1 tablespoon (15 mL) pistachio oil or extra-virgin olive oil

¼ cup (60 mL) toasted pistachios, chopped (see Toasted Nuts, page 290)

1 cup (250 mL) finely grated pecorino cheese

I grew up eating Brussels sprouts that had been boiled to an anemic state, each with a deep "X" cut into its base. It wasn't until I was a student in New York and tried my first deep-fried Brussels sprout at a David Chang restaurant that I realized I had been missing out on an incredibly versatile and flavourful vegetable. Although this recipe sidesteps the deep fryer, cooking the Brussels sprouts in a cast iron skillet really brings out their texture and nuttiness. Lemon and pecorino cheese make this dish bright, and adding pistachios makes it so craveable and moreish that it never lasts long.

In a medium cast iron skillet, heat about half of the neutral oil over high heat, until it starts to shimmer. Add about half of the Brussels sprouts and sprinkle with about half of the salt. Let the sprouts caramelize over high heat without stirring for 1 to 2 minutes, reducing the heat if they start to look too dark. Stir once. Continue to cook for an additional 1 to 2 minutes until the sprouts are charred but still crunchy. Transfer the sprouts to a large bowl or platter. Repeat with the remaining oil, Brussels sprouts, and salt.

In a small bowl, whisk together the Dijon, chilies, lemon juice, and pistachio oil. Drizzle the mixture over the sprouts. Add the pistachios and about half of the pecorino. Toss well to combine. Top with the remaining pecorino. Serve immediately.

Store leftovers in an airtight container in the fridge for up to 4 days.

# Fresh Peas with Bacon, Mint, and Burrata

**Serves 4**

2 tablespoons (30 mL) unsalted butter
2 slices thick-cut bacon
1 small white onion, thinly sliced
2 cups (500 mL) fresh or frozen peas
1 lemon, peeled and segmented
1 red long chili, thinly sliced
Salt and cracked black pepper
8 ounces (225 g) burrata cheese
Large handful of fresh mint

Peas are hands down the cutest vegetable, which is maybe why my kids love them and want them in everything. Peas in pasta, peas in soup, peas in pot pies. Peas everywhere. This is the recipe I make when I want a grown-up pea dish and something that has a bit of rugged sophistication to it. Fresh peas are always ideal, but the window for good ones is short and this dish is also great when you're looking for something bright in the dead of winter. You can use frozen peas for this recipe without any great loss in taste. A hearty slice of toast drizzled in fruity extra-virgin olive oil makes a great accompaniment to this dish, as does a poached egg or even, on an evening when you feel so inclined, Lamb Loin Chops over Minty Pistachio Butter (page 231).

In a large skillet or Dutch oven, heat the butter over medium-high heat until it is foamy. Add the bacon and reduce the heat to medium. Cook the bacon, flipping occasionally, until the fat has rendered and it is crisp, about 5 to 7 minutes. Transfer the bacon to a clean plate.

In the same skillet, cook the onion over medium-high heat for about 4 minutes until it has softened, stirring so it does not brown. Reduce the heat to low. Add the peas, stir, and cover. Cook for 4 to 5 minutes, until the peas are bright green and no longer have a raw taste. Turn off the heat. Chop the bacon and add it to the peas along with the lemon segments and chili. Season with salt and pepper to taste.

Working over the skillet to catch any drips, tear the burrata into 2-inch (5 cm) pieces. Add the burrata to the peas and top with the mint. Serve warm.

Store leftovers in an airtight container in the fridge for up to 4 days.

# A Note about Ready-Made Foods

I don't feel like cooking every night. There. I said it. I know, I know: this is a cookbook and maybe you were expecting me to tell you to roll up your sleeves, strap on a leather-trimmed apron, and spend thirty-six hours poaching a large piece of meat in a plastic bag under water, but that just isn't how or why I cook. I cook because I love food. Being playful and combining different ingredients and flavours in new ways bring a level of excitement to my day, but I also love doing other things that aren't cooking, and now more than ever it's important to support local restaurants, producers, and farms. Cooking is great! It's creative and inspiring and, for many of us, relaxing. But you know what else is great? Szechuan takeout! Tamales from your local bodega! One of those giant sheet-tray lasagnas that are actually kind of janky, but you didn't have to do anything but stick it in the oven, so who cares? Making ready-made food the centrepiece of your meal is totally okay. Often, when hosting others, I'll give myself a break and combine a few homemade dishes with store-bought ones and some thoughtful condiments. It's all so much *easier* and more *enjoyable* for everyone, and that's kind of the whole point of eating together, isn't it?

# Warm Beet Greens in Chicken Skin Vinaigrette

**Serves 4**

½ cup (125 mL) raw chicken skins
Salt and cracked black pepper
1 large bunch beet greens
2 cloves garlic, smashed
1 tablespoon (15 mL) Dijon mustard
2 tablespoons (30 mL) red wine vinegar

I try to put a bit of extra love into ingredients that typically get discarded. When most people buy a healthy-looking bunch of beets, they only want the beets. But what if I told you there was an added bonus? Often overlooked, beet greens are similar in flavour to Swiss chard with dark leafy greens and an earthy flavour. Chicken skin is another ingredient I use in this recipe that often goes to waste. While I might remove it if I'm braising or adding the chicken to a soup, I always save the skin. You can simply freeze it in a small airtight container and repurpose it as I do here: render it down, use the fat in lieu of oil to cook the greens, and use the crisped chicken skin as a sort of "crouton" to add a bit of texture.

Line a plate with paper towels. Roughly chop the chicken skins into 1-inch (2.5 cm) strips. In a medium cast iron skillet over medium heat, cook the chicken skins for 10 to 15 minutes, until the fat has rendered out and the skins become crispy. Using a slotted spoon, transfer the skins to the prepared plate. Season with salt and pepper to taste.

Thoroughly wash the beet greens. Trim off the stems 1 inch (2.5 cm) above where they meet the beets. Roughly chop the leafy parts into bite-size pieces. Cut the remaining stems into 2-inch (5 cm) pieces.

Place the same skillet you used to cook the chicken skins over medium-high heat. Add the beet stems and garlic. Cook for 2 to 3 minutes, until the stems and garlic soften. Add the leafy parts of the beet greens and stir so that they start to wilt. Continue cooking for another 5 minutes, until the greens are tender. Turn off the heat.

In a small bowl, whisk together the Dijon and vinegar. Pour the vinegar mixture over the greens and toss to coat. Break up any large pieces of chicken skin and sprinkle them over the greens. Serve immediately.

Store leftovers in an airtight container in the fridge for up to 5 days, but note that the skins will not stay crispy!

# Roasted Radishes with Horseradish

**Serves 4**

2 bunches red radishes with tops
2 tablespoons (30 mL) unsalted butter
Salt and cracked black pepper
Juice of ½ lemon
1-inch (2.5 cm) piece of fresh horseradish

I love a husky, spicy raw radish, but cooking them mellows out their flavour and they go a bit nutty. Waking them up with a squeeze of lemon and a flurry of horseradish brings a contrasting brightness. This is such a fun little side to put out next to Hot Honey Roast Chicken (page 210) or Herb Stuffed Rainbow Trout (page 200).

Use a sharp knife to remove the tops from the radishes. If the tops are already clean, set them aside, but if they aren't, plunge them into a large bowl of cold water to loosen any remaining grit. Drain. Cut the radishes in half.

In a large skillet over medium-high heat, melt the butter until it starts to foam. Add the radishes, cut side down, so that they all lie flat in the pan and have enough space to caramelize. (You may need to cook them in batches if you don't have a large enough skillet.) Season liberally with salt and pepper. Cook the radishes for 3 to 4 minutes, until golden brown. Flip them over and use a large spoon to baste them with the butter. Cook for 1 to 2 minutes until they are easily pierced with a paring knife. Using a slotted spoon, transfer them to a large plate. Do not wipe out the skillet or adjust the heat.

Shake any excess water off the radish tops. Tear any large pieces into bite-size pieces. Add the greens to the hot skillet and stir briefly until they soften and turn bright green, about 1 minute. Turn off the heat and return the radishes to the skillet. Season with the lemon juice and toss to combine.

Transfer the radishes and greens to a platter and, using a microplane, grate a flurry of horseradish over the whole thing. Serve immediately.

Store leftovers in an airtight container in the fridge for up to 4 days.

# Charred Corn with Peaches and Treviso

**Serves 4 to 6**

1 tablespoon (15 mL) + ¼ cup (60 mL) neutral oil, such as grapeseed or canola, divided

4 ears of corn, kernels removed and cobs discarded

Pinch of salt

1 teaspoon (5 mL) sweet paprika

1 small head of Treviso radicchio, leaves separated

4 ounces (115 g) goat cheese, crumbled

2 medium ripe peaches, diced

Pinch of ground red chilies

Juice of 2 limes

1 green long chili, sliced

Large handful of fresh mint, chopped

¼ cup (60 mL) Crispy Shallots (page 287)

Bitter greens like Treviso add both complexity and bite wherever they go. When they are combined with things that are a bit sweet and a bit creamy, as Treviso is here with charred corn, peaches, and goat cheese, they liven up the flavour party and highlight the best features of everything around them. Treviso has such a beautiful, deep purple colour that also makes this salad striking to look at. If you can't find Treviso, you can always substitute radicchio or even Belgian endive and I guarantee this salad will still be everything you need it to be on a hot summer day with a bottle of icy Sancerre or maybe a gin and tonic with heaps of lime. It does not matter if the corn is particularly hot or particularly cold for this recipe, and my approach is to get everything else ready and then assemble the salad when I find the corn to be the perfect, ambient temperature.

In a large skillet or Dutch oven over high heat, warm 1 tablespoon (15 mL) of the oil until it shimmers. Add the corn, but do not stir. Season with the salt and paprika and let cook for 2 to 3 minutes, until slightly charred. Stir, and cook for 1 minute more. Remove from the heat.

Place the Treviso, goat cheese, peaches, and corn in a large bowl. Add the red chilies. Drizzle with the remaining ¼ cup (60 mL) oil and the lime juice. Toss to combine.

Top with the green chili and fresh mint. This salad can hang around on the counter for 1 to 2 hours, if needed. If you don't plan to serve the salad immediately, hold off on garnishing it with the crispy shallots until just before you put it out.

Store leftovers in an airtight container in the fridge for up to 4 days. The shallots will lose their crunch, but the salad will still be good to eat.

# Braised Red Cabbage with Cider and Bacon

**Serves 4 to 6**

4 slices thick-cut bacon
1 medium yellow onion, thinly sliced
¼ cup (60 mL) light brown sugar
½ cup (125 mL) dry apple cider
½ cup (125 mL) apple cider vinegar
1 small red cabbage, thinly sliced
Salt and cracked black pepper

As a twentysomething, I deposited all my savings in an international bank account, loaded up a large, battered backpack, and got on a one-way flight to Germany. I wanted not just to see more of the world but to experience different tastes as well. Much of my time was spent visiting museums and walking the streets of Amsterdam, Berlin, Paris, Brussels, and Luxembourg, but also dining alone in cheap restaurants pretending I could somehow use cutlery and hold a paperback simultaneously. From the outside, these travels may have seemed a bit frivolous, but it was important to me to be a better cook and to expand what I knew about food. I tried to eat everything, even when I couldn't read the menu. Some dishes, like this simple dish of red cabbage braised in bacon fat that was served at a tiny restaurant in the Old Town in Prague, were a surprise when they landed on the table. Eating this dish was a touchstone moment that I'm convinced began my love affair with cabbage. Although my own recipe has evolved over the years, it reflects both the cozy feeling of a chilly night in Eastern Europe and the grounding feeling of a dish that stands the test of time.

Heat a large Dutch oven over medium-high heat. Add the bacon and cook until the fat has rendered and the bacon is crisp, about 5 to 6 minutes. Transfer the bacon to a clean plate.

Add the onion to the bacon fat and cook for 2 to 3 minutes, stirring occasionally, until softened. Sprinkle in the brown sugar and whisk until it dissolves. Add the apple cider and vinegar. Continue cooking for about 2 to 3 minutes, until the liquid is reduced by half. Add the cabbage and stir until it is evenly coated in the liquid. Increase the heat to high and bring to a boil. Cover, reduce the heat to low, and simmer for 20 to 30 minutes, until tender. Tear the bacon into bite-size pieces and add it to the cabbage. Season with salt and pepper to taste. Serve warm.

Store leftovers in an airtight container in the fridge for up to 4 days.

# Crispy Potatoes over Creamy Tonnato

**Serves 4 to 6**

### Tonnato

2 cans (3 ounces/85 g each) tuna, packed in extra-virgin olive oil

2 egg yolks

Zest and juice of 1 lemon

1 teaspoon (5 mL) fish sauce

1 clove garlic, smashed

½ cup (125 mL) extra-virgin olive oil

### Crispy Potatoes

3 to 4 starchy potatoes, such as Idaho or russet

½ cup (125 mL) neutral oil, for frying

Salt

### To serve

1 small bunch fresh flat-leaf parsley, chopped

1 tablespoon (15 mL) pickled long chilies, plus 1 tablespoon (15 mL) of their brine (page 291)

1 tablespoon (15 mL) extra-virgin olive oil

Salt and cracked black pepper

Tonnato is a Mediterranean condiment—a mayonnaise/aioli made from eggs, lemon, oil and good-quality canned tuna. Does fish purée sound weird to you? Maybe. And hey, I get that on an intellectual level, but on a basic "does this taste amazing?" level, I can assure you, it's very good. This recipe is fish forward, due to the addition of fish sauce, and pairs so well with crispy, chunky potatoes and the subtle spice of some fresh parsley. Although you can go to great lengths to explain how the dish comes together to whomever you are eating with, I find the best thing is just to put it on the table and watch it disappear.

**Make the Tonnato:** Place the tuna, egg yolks, lemon zest and juice, fish sauce, and garlic in a high-speed blender and pulse to combine. With the blender running on low speed, slowly stream in the olive oil until combined.

**Make the Crispy Potatoes:** Place the potatoes in a large saucepan of salted water over high heat. Bring the water to a boil. Reduce the heat to medium and cook at a gentle boil for 20 to 25 minutes, until the potatoes are easily pierced with a paring knife. Drain and set aside for about 5 minutes, until the potatoes are cool enough to handle. Using a fork, split the potatoes into roughly 2-inch (5 cm) chunks.

Set a large cast iron skillet over high heat. Add the oil and once it starts to shimmer, carefully add the potato chunks. Reduce the heat to medium so that the potatoes crisp but do not burn. Fry the potatoes for 4 to 7 minutes, turning them occasionally, until all sides are evenly browned. Salt generously.

**To serve:** In a medium bowl, place the parsley, chilies and brine, and olive oil. Season with salt and pepper to taste. Toss to combine.

Spoon the tonnato onto a large plate or platter. Place the crispy potatoes over the sauce. Top with the parsley mixture and serve immediately.

Store leftovers in an airtight container in the fridge for up to 4 days.

# On Potatoes

There comes a time when you must make and then immediately eat food that is solid and good and reaffirms that you are, in fact, still here. I say "a time," but actually this will happen many times over your life. I am sorry, but it's true. This may be after a breakup, when you find yourself in the eighth month of a pandemic, or simply at the end of a bad head cold. It could even be a horrific combination of all three. At that point, I will say to you what I have said to myself: "Cook a potato."

You cannot scrub a potato without having both feet firmly planted on the ground. Your hands must grip its rugged, knobby skin, and the smell of the earth will fill your nose. These are all very good things. It's a meditation of sorts, but a meditation where you end up with a hot meal at the end. I will not tell you how to cook your potato, because that is a personal choice, but I will tell you how I cook my potato when I am in need of one.

I like to get a nice big russet and prick it many times with a fork before setting the oven at about 450°F (230°C). I rub the potato all over with olive oil, sprinkle it generously with kosher salt, and then set it on a wire rack over a sheet tray and bake it for about 20 minutes until its skin has wrinkled and it has softened slightly. Then I pull it out of the oven and rub it all over again, but this time with unsalted butter. I turn the oven up to 475°F (240°C) and return the potato to the wire rack for another 20 minutes until it's crispy and, when squeezed gently with an oven-mitted hand, it yields.

After the potato cools slightly, I find a small, sharp knife and cut a line from one end of the potato to the other. There is something soothing about the precision of this ritual. There is also a sense of excitement because I am opening a package. The package, if cooked correctly, is full of warm, fluffy potato insides that I fluff even more with a fork, so that the steam billows out with all of the good smells. A potato needs very little at this point but depending on my mood I will add more butter and some crystals of flakey salt. If I truly need reminding that I *will* get through whatever is making me feel that I simply *can't*, I will add crème fraîche and a tin of cod.

It is a small, beautiful thing to give yourself a potato, and to allow whatever is taking up real estate in your brain to drift away on a cloud of warm, earthy steam. A potato will remind you that you are capable not just of cooking something perfectly, but of being resilient too. It is a celebration of your own steadfastness, your ability to take a knock and come back a little wiser, a little more tenacious than before. Sometimes life is hard in ways you don't always see coming. But think of all the potatoes out there, just waiting to be a comfort.

# Roasted Parsnips with Bacon Vinaigrette and Blue Cheese

**Serves 4**

1 pound (450 g) parsnips

2 tablespoons (30 mL) neutral oil, such as grapeseed or canola

1 teaspoon (5 mL) salt

2 slices thick-cut bacon, chopped

1 tablespoon (15 mL) pure maple syrup

2 tablespoons (30 mL) apple cider vinegar

¼ cup (60 mL) pecans, toasted and roughly chopped (see Toasted Nuts, page 290)

4 ounces (115 g) Stilton blue cheese, crumbled

Cracked black pepper

Parsnips get a bad rap and, to be fair, they can be kind of anemic tasting if they aren't treated right. I like to roast them hard to concentrate their flavour and then pair them with a savoury-sweet vinaigrette. Loaded up with bacon, toasted pecans, and blue cheese, this dish never fails to convince people that parsnips deserve love too.

Preheat the oven to 475°F (240°C). Line a baking sheet with parchment paper.

Cut any large parsnips in half, lengthwise. Place the parsnips in a large bowl. Add the oil and salt and toss to coat evenly. Spread the parsnips out on the prepared baking sheet. Roast for 10 to 15 minutes, until the parsnips are charred on the outside and easily pierced with a paring knife.

In a large cast iron skillet over medium-low heat, cook the bacon for about 5 to 7 minutes, until the fat is rendered and the bacon is crisp. Turn off the heat and immediately swirl in the maple syrup and vinegar. Add the cooked parsnips and gently toss to coat.

Transfer the parsnips to a platter. Top with the pecans, blue cheese, and a few grinds of black pepper. Serve immediately.

Leftovers are more delicious than you'd expect and can be stored in an airtight container in the fridge for up to 3 days.

# Paprika Sweet Potatoes with Lime Crema

**Serves 4 to 6**

If my daughters planned our menu, we would eat potatoes and sour cream for dinner every night. Unfortunately for them, I like variety, but fortunately for them, I'm willing to meet them in the middle if we mix it up a little. I like this recipe because it's an easy sell to five-year-olds, and it is a bit more interesting to me because of the spicy harissa and zippy lime.

### Sweet Potatoes

4 medium sweet potatoes

2 tablespoons (30 mL) extra-virgin olive oil

Pinch of salt

1 tablespoon (15 mL) sweet paprika

2 tablespoons (30 mL) Harissa (page 296)

### Crema

½ cup (125 mL) full-fat sour cream

Zest and juice of 1 lime

1 cup (250 mL) fresh cilantro, roughly chopped

Preheat the oven to 475°F (240°C). Line a rimmed baking sheet with parchment paper.

**Make the Sweet Potatoes:** Cut each sweet potato into 8 wedges. If your sweet potatoes are truly huge, you might want to cut each one in half around the equator and then cut each half into 8 wedges. Each wedge should be about 1 × 4 inches (2.5 × 10 cm). Place the sweet potatoes in a medium bowl and drizzle with the olive oil. Season with the salt and paprika. Toss to combine.

Spread the sweet potatoes in a single layer on the prepared baking sheet and roast for 15 to 20 minutes, until they are charred and easily pierced with a paring knife. Remove the potatoes from the oven and drizzle with the harissa.

**Make the Crema:** In a small bowl, place the sour cream. Add the lime zest and juice. Stir to combine.

**To serve:** Transfer the potatoes to a serving dish. Serve the crema alongside the potatoes or even dollop it on top. Garnish with the cilantro. Serve immediately.

Store leftover potatoes in an airtight container in the fridge for up to 4 days. Store leftover crema in an airtight container in the fridge for up to 5 days.

# Caramelized Fennel with Citrus and Parmesan

**Serves 4**

3 heads of fennel

2 teaspoons (10 mL) salt

1 to 2 tablespoons (15 to 30 mL) neutral oil, such as grapeseed or canola

½ cup (125 mL) dry white wine

2 cups (500 mL) low-sodium chicken stock

Small handful of fresh thyme sprigs, tied

Juice of 1 large orange

2 ounces (55 g) Parmesan cheese

½ cup (125 mL) large Bread Crumbs (page 289)

Some vegetables are best served raw, and some are greatly enhanced by a little cookery. A select few vegetables are good either way, and it's impossible to get them wrong. Fennel is one of these very special vegetables. While I'm always happy to see it raw—crunchy and with a hint of licorice flavour, hanging out on a crudité platter or alongside Salt Cod Brandade with Herb Salad (page 25)—I also love it cooked because it becomes wonderfully mellow and still maintains some of its texture. Fennel and citrus are a classic combo, and in this dish they really shine together.

Cut the fennel in half, core it, and remove any tough outer leaves. Cut each half into 3 wedges and season with the salt.

Line a plate with paper towels. In a large Dutch oven over medium-high heat, heat 1 tablespoon (15 mL) of the oil. Working in batches, brown the fennel on all sides, about 2 to 3 minutes per side, reducing the heat and/or adding more oil if it starts to smoke. Transfer the fennel to the prepared plate. Once all the fennel has been browned, wipe out any remaining oil with paper towel.

With the Dutch oven over medium-high heat, add the white wine. Using a wooden spoon, scrape any browned bits off the bottom. Add the fennel. Add the chicken stock, thyme, and orange juice. Reduce the heat to medium, cover, and let the fennel braise for 15 to 20 minutes, until tender.

Meanwhile, preheat the oven to 425°F (220°C).

Once the fennel is tender, use a slotted spoon to transfer it to a clean plate. Increase the heat to high to reduce the braising liquid. Continue cooking over high heat until about 1 cup (250 mL) of liquid remains in the Dutch oven. Return the fennel to the liquid. Top with the Parmesan and bread crumbs. Bake for 7 to 10 minutes, until golden brown and bubbling. Let stand for about 5 minutes and then serve.

Store leftovers in an airtight container in the fridge for up to 4 days.

# Roasted Carrots with Tahini and Herbs

**Serves 4**

1 large bunch rainbow carrots, including tops

2 tablespoons (30 mL) extra-virgin olive oil, divided

1 teaspoon (5 mL) salt, more to taste

1 teaspoon (5 mL) ground sumac

Juice of 1 lemon, divided

½ cup (125 mL) Tahini Dip (page 294)

½ cup (125 mL) fresh mint, roughly chopped

½ cup (125 mL) fresh flat-leaf parsley, roughly chopped

2 tablespoons (30 mL) toasted sesame seeds

Often, the fluffy green tops of carrots get lobbed off and dumped in the compost, but—especially when they are super fresh—I love to make use of them as well. They have such a good flavour: like a carrot, yes, but like a *green* carrot, which is less sweet and more herbal. These wonderful tops can be tossed into a pesto or a spicy zhoug, or quickly chopped and mixed with salad greens or herbs as they are here. This recipe is really about using the whole carrot and making a dish bursting with colour, texture, and flavour.

Preheat the oven to 425°F (220°C). Line a rimmed baking sheet with parchment paper or foil.

Remove the tops from the carrots. Trim off the stems, leaving only the fluffy fronds at the top, and set aside about 1 cup (250 mL) of the nicest ones. Cut the carrots in half lengthwise and place them in a medium bowl. Add 1 tablespoon (15 mL) of the olive oil, the salt, and the sumac. Toss to coat evenly. Arrange the carrots on the prepared baking sheet. Roast for 15 to 20 minutes, until they are easily pierced with a fork.

Place a quarter of the roasted carrots in a high-speed blender. Add about half of the lemon juice. Pulse to combine. Add the tahini dip. Purée until smooth.

Tear the carrot tops into bite-size pieces and place them in a small bowl. Add the mint and parsley. Season with salt to taste. Add the remaining 1 tablespoon (15 mL) olive oil and the remaining lemon juice. Toss to combine.

Spoon the tahini mixture onto a large plate and spread it around. Arrange the roasted carrots on top. Top with the herb salad and sprinkle with the sesame seeds.

Store leftovers in an airtight container in the fridge for up to 5 days.

# Hominy Cab 'n' Cheese

**Serves 4**

3 tablespoons (45 mL) unsalted butter, divided

2 cups (500 mL) shredded green or Savoy cabbage

2 tablespoons (30 mL) all-purpose flour

1½ cups (375 mL) whole milk (3.25%), warm

1 tablespoon (15 mL) Dijon mustard

Pinch of ground nutmeg

½ cup (125 mL) shredded sharp white cheddar cheese

½ cup (125 mL) shredded Emmental or Swiss cheese

½ cup (125 mL) shredded Parmesan cheese

Salt and cracked black pepper

1 can (25 ounces/700 g) hominy, drained and rinsed

2 cups (500 mL) large Bread Crumbs (page 289)

When it comes to making macaroni and cheese for my daughters, sometimes boiling the noodles is just an extra step I don't have time for. Invention is the necessity of all mothers, and hominy—giant kernels of maize soaked in lime and ready to eat in a can—is a great, quick substitution for noodles in baked pasta dishes. In fact, hominy may just be superior to pasta in this application because hominy (unlike pasta) doesn't swell in the sauce or become "sauce-logged," and has just a slight bite to it, which is great in a creamy sauce alongside fried cabbage and some crunchy bread crumbs. Even though this dish is not typical, it has quickly become a go-to in our household on busy nights when I want to get a hot meal on the table without too much effort.

Preheat the oven to 400°F (200°C). Lightly grease a 9-inch (2.5 L) square baking dish.

In a large Dutch oven over medium-high heat, melt 1 tablespoon (15 mL) of the butter. Once it starts to get foamy, add the cabbage and sauté until just cooked, about 5 to 7 minutes. Transfer to a medium bowl and set aside.

In the same Dutch oven you used to cook the cabbage, melt the remaining 2 tablespoons (30 mL) butter over medium-high heat. Sprinkle in the flour and whisk the mixture continuously for 2 to 3 minutes until a thick paste forms, making sure it does not scorch or stick to the Dutch oven. Whisk in the warm milk and continue cooking for another 5 minutes to make a thick sauce. Turn off the heat. Add the Dijon, nutmeg, cheddar, Emmental, and Parmesan and stir until the cheese melts. Season with salt and pepper to taste. Add the cabbage and hominy to the cheese mixture. Stir to combine.

Transfer the mixture to the prepared baking dish. Sprinkle with the bread crumbs. Bake, uncovered, for 15 to 20 minutes until golden and bubbling.

Leftovers can be eaten hot or cold. Store them in an airtight container in the fridge for up to 5 days.

# Butternut Squash and Sharp Cheddar Gratin

**Serves 4 to 6**

1 medium butternut squash,
  cut into 2-inch (5 cm) cubes

1 cup (250 mL) heavy (35%) cream

2 cloves garlic, smashed

1 teaspoon (5 mL) salt

1 teaspoon (5 mL) Aleppo pepper

1 small bundle of fresh thyme sprigs

1 cup (250 mL) shredded sharp
  cheddar cheese

½ cup (125 mL) Bread Crumbs
  (page 289)

Butternut squash can be somehow both sweet and bland if it's simply steamed, but when you cook it gently in cream and then smother it in a sharp cheddar sauce and bread crumbs, it is always delicious. The nice thing about a gratin is that it isn't too involved to make. You can even prepare it well in advance and leave it in the oven for a few extra minutes, until you're ready to serve it. This makes it enjoyable not just for the eater but also for the cooker. This recipe in particular—based loosely on a recipe by my friend Jason Alley—is a snap to put together and never fails to deliver on all critical gratin merits (Creamy! Bubbly! Crunchy top!). I use plain ol' homemade bread crumbs on my version, but the original calls for crushed Ritz crackers, which, should you be the sort of person who likes things a bit "extra," I fully endorse.

Preheat the oven to 425°F (220°C).

In a medium saucepan over medium-high heat, place the squash, cream, garlic, salt, Aleppo, and thyme. Bring to a boil, then reduce the heat to low. Simmer, covered, for 20 to 25 minutes, until the squash is tender. Using a slotted spoon, transfer the squash to a 13- × 9-inch (3.5 L) baking dish.

Fish the thyme sprigs out of the cream mixture remaining in the saucepan and discard. Smash the garlic so it blends into the sauce. Increase the heat to medium-high. Cook the cream for 5 minutes, stirring constantly to prevent it from scorching. Turn off the heat. Stir in the cheddar until melted.

Pour the cheddar cream over the squash. Sprinkle the bread crumbs overtop. Bake for 15 to 20 minutes, until hot and bubbling. Serve hot.

Store leftovers in an airtight container in the fridge for up to 4 days.

# Tartiflette

**Serves 4**

2½ pounds (1.125 kg) starchy potatoes, such as Idaho or russet

Salt

1 tablespoon (15 mL) extra-virgin olive oil

2 medium yellow onions, thinly sliced

1 clove Garlic Confit (page 286)

½ cup (125 mL) dry white wine

½ cup (125 mL) heavy (35%) cream

¼ pound (115 g) speck or prosciutto, thinly sliced

12 ounces (340 g) reblochon cheese or aged brie

My friend Rossy Earle made this classic après-ski dish of speck (thinly sliced smoked pork), onions, potatoes, and cheese for a party. While I've never been one to shy away from a casserole, I attempted to take a modest portion so that there would be enough to go around. I don't want to be dramatic, but practising restraint was agony. Not everyone noticed the bubbling tartiflette that kept wafting hot potato fog at me. I dove in and certainly took more than my share. I still dream about this dish, especially in the cooler months when I've been running around outside and want to come in, put on a fresh pair of woolly socks, and just get hygge with it.

Place the whole potatoes in a large saucepan and cover with cold water. Salt it until it tastes like the sea, then bring it to a boil over high heat. Reduce the heat to medium and cook the potatoes for 18 to 20 minutes, just until they are easily pierced with a paring knife. Drain the potatoes. Set aside until they are cool enough to handle.

Place a medium skillet over high heat. Add the olive oil and onions. Cook for 2 to 3 minutes, stirring frequently until softened. Add the garlic confit. Use a spoon to break it up a bit. Continue stirring for another 2 to 3 minutes, until the onions are soft. Add the wine. Continue cooking until the wine reduces by half. Turn off the heat but leave the skillet on the element. Pour in the cream and stir to combine.

Preheat the oven to 400°F (200°C).

Using your hands, break up the potatoes into large chunks. Lay about one third of the potatoes snugly in the bottom of an 11- × 7-inch (2 L) ovenproof dish. Nestle about one third of the speck into the potatoes, distributing it more or less evenly on the casserole. Place about one third of the onion mixture overtop. Repeat this process twice until you've used all the potatoes, speck, and onion mixture. Slice the cheese and place it in an even layer on top. Bake for 20 to 25 minutes, until the tartiflette it is hot and bubbling. Serve immediately.

Leftovers can be stored in an airtight container in the fridge for up to 3 days.

# A Centre of Vegetables

**Pick a vegetable that makes your mouth water and plan a meal around it.**

In her book *More Home Cooking*, Laurie Colwin writes, "Our tables still feature the large piece of meat, the potato and some vegetables which are very much an afterthought. What would happen if the vegetables were the first thought?" I wish that Laurie and I had met and that I could have had her over to dinner. I would have served her a table brimming with recipes like Roasted Butternut Squash with Labneh and Pistachios (page 138), Fried Cheese Salad (page 117), Spicy Oven Charred Cabbage and Lemons (page 152), and even Green Lasagna (page 167). In this section, vegetables are the first thought, and they are at the centre of the table.

That's not to say you'll find only vegetables in this chapter. There are dishes to appeal to a range of palates, including Prosciutto Wrapped Eggplant (page 142), Green Gazpacho with Salmon and Cucumber (page 125), and Sauerkraut Soup (page 129). Vegetables are, without compromise, the star of the show here. Sometimes this happens in familiar ways, as with Lentil Soup (page 130) or Grilled Vegetable Salad with Maple Balsamic Dressing (page 122), but vegetables also take the spotlight in ways that are delightful in their novelty, such as Fried Cabbage with Halloumi and Jalapenos (page 151) and Pumpkin Stuffed Shells with Brown Butter Béchamel (page 165).

However you like your vegetables—raw, roasted, blanched, or fried—there is a recipe for you in this section. You might want to put together a very easy and very moreish Jammy Tomatoes and Butter Bean Bake (page 137) and then perhaps head to another section of the book for something to go with it, such as Harissa Chicken (page 213) or Tomato Roasted Salmon (page 204), or even grab a few sides from your favourite takeout spot and have a meal that is full of vegetables but also gentle for you to put together.

# Asparagus, Poached Eggs, and Crispy Prosciutto

**Serves 4 to 6**

6 slices prosciutto

2 bunches asparagus

¼ cup (60 mL) white vinegar

6 eggs

¼ cup (60 mL) extra-virgin olive oil

Juice of 1 lemon

½ cup (125 mL) Bread Crumbs (page 289)

Salt and cracked black pepper

Looking at the ingredients list, it doesn't seem like there's much to this dish. But the more you eat it, the more you will find reasons to keep eating it. There are a lot of lovely textures, eggs that begin to sauce the dish when you poke their yolks, and just enough acidity to keep things lively.

Preheat the oven to 325°F (160°C). Line a rimmed baking sheet with parchment paper.

Place the prosciutto slices on the prepared baking sheet. Bake for 15 minutes, until crispy. Transfer the prosciutto to a wire rack to cool.

Bring a large saucepan of salted water to a boil. While you're waiting for the water to boil, fill a medium bowl halfway with water and ice.

Working in batches, drop about a quarter of the asparagus into the boiling water and stir once to make sure all the spears are submerged. Blanch the asparagus until bright green and crisp-tender, about 3 to 5 minutes depending on the thickness of the asparagus. Using tongs, lift the spears out of the saucepan and immediately plunge them into the prepared bowl of ice water to chill. Bring the water back to a boil and repeat until all of the asparagus has been blanched. Do not discard the water. You can use it to poach the eggs.

Drain the asparagus, then use a clean kitchen towel to dry it. Transfer the asparagus to a large plate or platter.

Add the vinegar to the boiling water. Reduce the heat to low so that it holds a simmer. Gently crack each egg into its own small dish or ramekin to ensure that the yolk does not break and there are no loose bits of shell. Carefully lower the eggs into the water and cook for 4 minutes. Using a slotted spoon, transfer the eggs to the plate with the asparagus.

Drizzle the asparagus and eggs with the olive oil and lemon juice. Break apart the prosciutto and place it on top. Sprinkle the bread crumbs overtop. Season with salt and pepper to taste. Serve immediately.

Store leftovers in an airtight container in the fridge for up to 2 days.

# Minty Smashed Chickpea and Plum Freekeh Salad

**Serves 6 to 8**

1 cup (250 mL) freekeh

1½ teaspoons (7 mL) + 1½ tablespoons (22 mL) walnut oil, divided, more for drizzling

Pinch of salt, more to taste

1 can (14 ounces/400 mL) chickpeas, drained and rinsed

4 plums, pitted and diced

Zest and juice of 1 lemon

1 cup (250 mL) loosely packed fresh mint, roughly chopped

1 cup (250 mL) loosely packed fresh flat-leaf parsley, roughly chopped

2 teaspoons (10 mL) Aleppo pepper

Modern families are wonderful but complicated to explain. My daughters' grandad, Samy, is not technically my father-in-law but he more or less is my father-in-law. Samy does the things a traditional father-in-law would do like remember my birthday, babysit when I get in a jam, and give me well-considered advice. He is also an amazing cook with a ton of knowledge. "Not-marrying" into a Middle Eastern family has made my cooking so much better, and Samy is always recommending a book or an ingredient that I will diligently hunt down and try. Freekeh—a smoked green wheat from the Levant—is one of those ingredients. I've come to love its slightly smoky, nutty flavour and the fact that it's very easy to cook. Here, I've paired it with lots of herbs, which is typical, but also with plums and walnut oil, which makes for a really savoury-sweet grain salad that's hard to stop eating.

Cook the freekeh according to package instructions. Drain and place it in a large bowl. Drizzle with 1½ teaspoons (7 mL) of the walnut oil. Sprinkle with a generous pinch of salt. Fluff the freekeh with a fork and let cool to room temperature.

Place the chickpeas in a medium bowl and smash once or twice with a potato masher or the bottom of a metal measuring cup. Add the chickpeas to the bowl with the freekeh and drizzle with the remaining 1½ tablespoons (22 mL) walnut oil. Add the plums, lemon zest and juice, about half of the mint, half of the parsley, the Aleppo, and more salt to taste. Toss to combine. Top with the remaining mint and parsley and a drizzle of walnut oil. Serve immediately.

Store leftovers (which are delicious!) in an airtight container in the fridge for up to 4 days.

# White Lentil and Lime Salad

**Serves 4 to 5**

### Dressing

8 lime leaves

1 clove garlic, smashed

1 jalapeno pepper, stemmed and roughly chopped

1-inch (2.5 cm) piece of ginger, peeled and roughly chopped

Zest and juice of 2 limes (about ¼ cup/60 mL juice)

2 tablespoons (30 mL) pure liquid honey

⅓ cup (75 mL) neutral oil, such as canola or grapeseed

¼ cup (60 mL) soy sauce

### Lentils

2¼ cups (550 mL) water

1 cup (250 mL) dried white lentils

4 lime leaves

2 teaspoons (10 mL) ground turmeric

1 teaspoon (5 mL) salt

### Pickled Turnips

2 medium white turnips, peeled and cut into bite-size chunks

1 cup (250 mL) rice wine vinegar

1 tablespoon (15 mL) pure liquid honey

2 bags hibiscus tea

This is a toothsome big salad that can easily be prepped ahead of time and assembled at the last minute. Its vibrant colours brighten up any spread, and while the acidity and punch of the pickled turnips can be refreshing in warmer months, the lentils are such a wonderful option for cooler months when heartier fare is favoured. The dressing is one of my absolute favourites, care of Scott Vivian, who serves it as the house dressing at his restaurant Beast in Toronto. I've simplified it slightly for the home cook. The recipe makes a bit more dressing than you need for this salad, but it keeps well. In fact, I typically double the dressing recipe so I have it on hand to perk up leftover roasted vegetables or to drizzle over chicken or fish.

**Make the Dressing:** Place the lime leaves, garlic, jalapeno, ginger, lime zest and juice, and honey in a high-speed blender. Pulse to combine. With the blender running on high speed, drizzle in the oil and then the soy sauce. Continue blending until the lime leaves are broken down.

**Make the Lentils:** In a medium saucepan over high heat, place the water, lentils, lime leaves, turmeric, and salt. Once the water starts to simmer, reduce the heat to low, cover, and simmer gently for 17 minutes, stirring occasionally, or until the lentils are just tender. Turn off the heat and let the lentils stand for 5 minutes.

Fluff the lentils with a fork. Add 1 tablespoon (15 mL) of the dressing. Toss to coat evenly. Let the lentils cool to room temperature. Refrigerate until ready to use.

**Make the Pickled Turnips:** Place the turnips in a mason jar with a tight-fitting lid. In a small saucepan over high heat, place the vinegar, honey, and tea bags. Bring to a boil, pressing the tea bags with the back of a spoon to help release their colour. Remove the saucepan from the heat.

*recipe continues*

**Salad**

6 cups (1.5 L) mixed greens

½ cup (125 mL) fresh flat-leaf parsley, chopped

½ cup (125 mL) fresh mint, chopped, more to garnish

1 jalapeno, thinly sliced

Salt and cracked black pepper

1 cucumber, seeded and chopped

2 avocados, pitted, peeled, and sliced

Pour the brine over the turnips, pushing the turnips down in the jar to ensure that they are submerged. Firmly tighten the lid. Let the pickles cool to room temperature, turning the jar upside down every so often to ensure even distribution of the brine. Open the jar, fish out the tea bags, and discard. Transfer the turnips to the fridge and store there until ready to use.

**Make the Salad:** Place the mixed greens in a large bowl. Add the parsley, mint, and jalapeno. Season with salt and pepper to taste. Drizzle about ¾ cup (175 mL) of the dressing over the salad. Toss to combine. Top with the lentils, cucumber, avocado, pickled turnips, a few more sprigs of mint, and another drizzle of dressing.

# Dear Salad, Please Forgive Me (Plus a Formula of Sorts)

Salad and I got off to a rocky start. As a teen in the 1990s, I had very specific (and uninspired) ideas about what ought to comprise a salad: lettuce (likely romaine), some other raw vegetables that had been chopped or ribboned, and maybe a crouton or two. A salad was a collection of so-called "healthy" foods combined to make a new food, but not one that was necessarily composed or had a point of view.

Compounding this sad salad narrative was my first restaurant job. I had started as a baker and somehow got "promoted" from the day shift to the evening shift, which essentially meant that I had to work much harder and faster for the same amount of money and with a bunch of rowdy hormonal boy-men instead of the wise and empathetic head baker, Sandra. The restaurant was fancy, so fancy in fact that with your expensive entree (Blackened haddock! Duck breast with fig gastrique!) you were offered a complimentary all-you-can-eat salad bar. In my naiveté, I was thrilled to be offered the opportunity to lug Rubbermaid tubs full of ice down a flight of stairs, where I then heaved them into a large salad bar and spread a collection of "salads and stuff" overtop.

It would be years before I would reconsider what a salad was, exactly—that I would realize a salad could be made of all sorts of things, hot and cold, cooked and raw, plant and animal. A salad can be a collection of things, sure, but that collection of things, just like a soup or a stir-fry, still has to make sense and have a point of view. You can't just chuck a bunch of things and a handful of Craisins into a big wooden bowl, give it a toss, and expect it to taste cohesive. You have to think about it and compose a salad as you would any other dish.

Since that first restaurant job, I have developed what I believe is a foolproof formula for making a good salad. It requires the following:

Something...
- creamy: cheese, avocado, labneh, tahini or other nut butters
- vegetable-y: greens, raw vegetables, roasted vegetables, fruits, herbs
- crunchy: nuts, seeds, pita chips, crispy shallots, granola, bread crumbs, thinly sliced radishes
- oil-y: olive oil, canola oil, bacon fat, walnut oil, chili crisp, harissa, oil-packed tuna
- acidic/tart: citrus, vinegar, fruit juice, sumac, yogurt

That may seem like a lot of different things to put in one salad because, well, it is! There are so many great ways to combine flavours and textures into a dish that teenage me would not have recognized as a salad.

Do plums look good at the market? Toss them on a platter with some radicchio, walnuts, basil, and fried halloumi and then drizzle liberally with walnut oil and date vinegar.

Maybe you opened your fridge and all you have is an overripe canary melon and some condiments. Cut the melon into bite-size chunks and let it marinate in the fridge for an hour or so with a drizzle of olive oil, a glug of vinegar, and a tablespoon or two of soy sauce. Then spoon that onto a chilled plate covered in plain Greek yogurt and Hot Honey (page 293). Finish it off with a fistful of fresh garden herbs and pistachios, and voilà!

Even last night's leftover Prosciutto Wrapped Eggplant (page 142) can be reimagined on a bed of Tahini Dip (page 294) or even store-bought tzatziki with a few pita chips, fresh mint, and some chili oil.

To make an excellent salad, you don't need much in the way of skill or even ingredients, just a sense of possibility and, really, a little basic food math. By all means, follow the recipes in this book for really great salads, but when your imagination or a specific ingredient calls to you, don't be afraid to colour outside the lines to make something totally unique that you'll want to replicate again and again.

# Fried Cheese Salad

**Serves 4 to 6**

7 ounces (200 g) halloumi cheese, sliced about ½ inch (1 cm) thick

2 tablespoons (30 mL) extra-virgin olive oil, divided

2 bunches kale, washed and torn into bite-size pieces

Pinch of salt

3 cups (750 mL) soft fresh herbs, such as dill, mint, and flat-leaf parsley

1 lemon, quartered and thinly sliced with seeds removed

½ cup (125 mL) Tahini Dip (page 294)

¼ cup (60 mL) Dukkah (page 297)

I do not crave salad because it's healthy; I crave it because it tastes good. In fact, my only objective in making a salad is that it be as delicious as possible. This one definitely ticks that box. Pan-frying halloumi gives it a hit of saltiness, as well as some crispy edges. The kale, which gets massaged and then covered in herbs, Dukkah (page 297), and Tahini Dip (page 294), is the perfect hearty green to stand up to it. This is the kind of salad that makes people who hate kale come back for seconds, so don't hesitate to double the recipe.

Blot the halloumi slices dry with paper towels. Line a plate with fresh paper towels.

In a large skillet over high heat, warm about ½ tablespoon (7 mL) of the olive oil, until it just starts to shimmer. Lay the halloumi slices in the pan. Sear each side until golden brown, about 1 to 2 minutes per side. Transfer the seared halloumi to the prepared plate.

Place the kale in a large bowl. Drizzle with the remaining 1½ tablespoons (22 mL) olive oil. Add the salt. Using your hands, massage the kale until it is evenly coated in the oil and has softened.

Tear the halloumi into bite-size pieces. Add it to the bowl with the kale. Add the soft herbs, lemon slices, tahini dip, and dukkah. To avoid bruising the herbs, toss gently to combine. Make sure the kale is evenly coated. Serve immediately.

Store leftovers in an airtight container in the fridge for up to 2 days.

# Shoulder Season Salad

**Serves 4 to 6**

3 to 4 medium yellow beets

3 tablespoons (45 mL) extra-virgin olive oil, divided

Juice of 1 lemon, divided

Salt and cracked black pepper

1 head of butter lettuce, leaves separated

1 small head of radicchio, torn into bite-size pieces

½ medium bulb of fennel, thinly sliced

3 red radishes, thinly sliced

1 jalapeno, thinly sliced

1 cup (250 mL) fresh mint, roughly chopped

4 ounces (115 g) good-quality blue cheese, crumbled

Shoulder season is the time between peak seasons when the lines of spring and summer or fall and winter blur together and you can go from being overdressed to underdressed in the span of a few minutes. These are the moments when you need something a bit heartier than a summer salad, and this salad fits the bill. Crispy mint and lemon flavours contrast happily with beautiful earthy roasted beets, bitter radicchio, and some funky blue cheese. Serve it alongside Pan Seared Ribeyes with Ramp and Anchovy Butter (page 241), and if your beets come with some lovely big tops, whip up some Warm Beet Greens in Chicken Skin Vinaigrette (page 78) as well.

Preheat the oven to 475°F (240°C).

If your beets come with tops, cut them off and reserve for another use. Place the beets on a rimmed baking sheet. Roast for 40 to 50 minutes, until easily pierced with a paring knife. Set aside to cool.

When the beets are cool enough to handle, use a paring knife to peel them. Cut them into bite-size chunks. Drizzle with 1 tablespoon (15 mL) of the olive oil and half of the lemon juice. Season with salt and pepper to taste. Toss to combine.

Spread the butter lettuce leaves out on a large round plate or platter. Top with the radicchio, beets, fennel, radishes, jalapeno, and mint. Season with salt and pepper. Drizzle with the remaining 2 tablespoons (30 mL) olive oil and the remaining lemon juice. Top with the cheese. Serve immediately.

# Winter Panzanella Salad

**Serves 4 to 6**

1 small sugar pumpkin, peeled, seeded, and cut into 2-inch (5 cm) chunks

1 delicata squash, halved, seeded, and sliced 1 inch (2.5 cm) thick

2 to 3 shallots, halved

½ loaf stale bread, torn into bite-size chunks

1 bunch fresh sage, stems removed and discarded and leaves roughly chopped

2 tablespoons (30 mL) extra-virgin olive oil

2 pinches of salt, divided

Pinch of ground red chilies

1 tablespoon (15 mL) Hot Honey (page 293)

1 bunch kale, washed and torn into bite-size pieces

1 tablespoon (15 mL) hazelnut oil, more for drizzling

1 tablespoon (15 mL) red wine vinegar

8 ounces (225 g) bocconcini cheese

½ cup (125 mL) hazelnuts, toasted and roughly chopped (see Toasted Nuts, page 290)

A classic panzanella salad is made with ripe tomatoes and stale bread, and this is by no means a classic version. This delicious winter panzanella has all the good stale bread energy you're used to in a panzanella but also slightly charred and caramelized pumpkin and squash, tons of sage, and nutty hazelnuts. A hit of red wine vinegar and a little Hot Honey (page 293) carry this panzanella over the finish line.

Preheat the oven to 475°F (240°C). Line a large rimmed baking sheet with parchment paper.

In a large bowl, place the pumpkin, squash, shallots, bread, sage, olive oil, a pinch of salt, and the chilies. Toss to combine.

Spread the mixture in an even layer on the prepared baking sheet. Roast for 15 to 20 minutes, until the bread is slightly toasted and the pumpkin is easily pierced with a fork. Remove from the oven and drizzle with the hot honey. Stir briefly and set aside to cool while you prepare the other ingredients.

In the same large bowl you used to combine the vegetables and bread, place the kale. Add the hazelnut oil, red wine vinegar, and a pinch of salt. Massage the ingredients until the kale is evenly coated.

Check to make sure the vegetable and bread mixture is not hot; it should be warm or room temperature before you add it or the kale will wilt. Add the roasted vegetable and bread mixture and half of the cheese and hazelnuts to the kale. Toss to combine. Top the salad with the remaining cheese and hazelnuts and a drizzle of hazelnut oil.

This salad keeps relatively well. Store leftovers in an airtight container in the refrigerator for up to 4 days.

# Grilled Vegetable Salad with Maple Balsamic Dressing

**Serves 4 to 6**

When I'm cooking at home—especially in the summer—firing up the barbeque offers an opportunity to get outdoors and avoid turning on the stove. When I really want to get my grill on, I prepare this simple salad. Grilling vegetable is a lot more forgiving than grilling animal proteins. All you really need to do is get your grill smoking hot and leave your veggies on there just long enough to get grill marks, flip them, and mark them again. Any residual heat will finish the cooking for you while you get the other ingredients together and throw some bread on the still-hot grill to round out your meal.

## Salad

1 medium eggplant, sliced ¾ inch (2 cm) thick

1 tablespoon (15 mL) salt, more for seasoning

2 portobello mushrooms, sliced ¾ inch (2 cm) thick

1 medium zucchini, sliced ¾ inch (2 cm) thick

Cracked black pepper

1 bunch kale, washed and torn into bite-size pieces

1 small head of radicchio, chopped

4 ounces (115 g) goat cheese

Juice of 1 lemon

## Dressing

2 cloves garlic, smashed

Pinch of ground red chilies

¼ cup (60 mL) balsamic vinegar

2 tablespoons (30 mL) pure maple syrup

½ cup (125 mL) extra-virgin olive oil

**Start the Salad:** Place the eggplant in a colander. Toss with the salt and place the colander in the sink. Let the eggplant drain for about 20 minutes.

**Make the Dressing:** In a medium bowl, whisk together the garlic, chilies, vinegar, maple syrup, and olive oil.

**Finish the Salad:** Rinse the eggplant to remove the salt and pat dry with a clean kitchen towel or paper towels Place the eggplant, mushrooms, and zucchini in a shallow dish and pour about one third of the dressing on top. Flip the vegetables around a few times and let them soak up the dressing for about 30 minutes.

Heat the grill to high. Remove the vegetables from the marinade and discard it. Season the vegetables with salt and pepper. Using tongs, lay the vegetables on the grill. Let cook, undisturbed, for 2 to 3 minutes, until they have obvious grill marks. Flip and cook for an additional 2 to 3 minutes. Transfer the vegetables to a platter and let stand until they are cool enough to handle.

Place the kale, radicchio, and cheese in a large bowl. Chop the vegetables into bite-size pieces and add them to the bowl. Drizzle the lemon juice overtop. Pour on the remaining dressing and toss well to combine. Serve immediately.

Store leftovers in an airtight container in the fridge for up to 2 days.

# Green Gazpacho with Salmon and Cucumber

## Serves 4 to 6

**Poached Salmon**

6 ounces (170 g) salmon
Pinch of salt
5 lime leaves (optional)

**Gazpacho**

Juice of 4 limes
¼ cup (60 mL) fresh cilantro
¼ cup (60 mL) fresh basil
1 jalapeno, cored and chopped
1 Granny Smith apple, cored and chopped
2 large avocados, pitted and peeled
1 large seedless cucumber, chopped
¼ cup (60 mL) extra-virgin olive oil, more for drizzling
3 cups (750 mL) cold water
Salt

**To serve**

2 Persian cucumbers, sliced
2 scallions, sliced
Extra-virgin olive oil, for drizzling

Green gazpacho is the perfect summer dinner. It's green, it's cold, and it's delicious. This version brings in a touch of sweetness from the apple, as well as body from the avocado. The poached salmon is quick to make, but if you're short on time you can skip it and use canned salmon or trout instead—or even just a few extra slices of avocado. One thing that is almost effortless, but makes this dish better, is to put your bowls in the freezer an hour or so before you dish up the soup. Serving green gazpacho in an icy bowl is the sort of small, everyday luxury it's nice to indulge in.

**Make the Poached Salmon:** Line a small plate with paper towels. Season the salmon with the salt. Place it in a small saucepan (with a lid) with the lime leaves (if using) and cover with water. Place the saucepan over high heat and bring the water to a boil. Reduce the heat to low so that the water is just simmering. Cover and poach, until barely cooked through, about 3 to 5 minutes. Transfer the salmon to the prepared plate. Place it in the fridge until ready to use.

**Make the Gazpacho:** Place the lime juice, cilantro, basil, jalapeno, and apple in a high-speed blender. Pulse to combine. Add the avocados and cucumber. Pulse to combine. With the blender running on low speed, slowly stream in the olive oil and then the water, blending until smooth. Season with salt to taste. Place the gazpacho in the fridge to chill for at least 1 hour and, if you can, overnight. Chilling will improve the flavour and allow the gazpacho to become very cold.

**To serve:** Divide the gazpacho among bowls. Using your hands, break the salmon into bite-size chunks. Top the gazpacho with the salmon, cucumber slices, scallions, and a drizzle of olive oil.

Store leftovers in an airtight container in the fridge for up to 4 days.

# Summer Beet Borscht

**Serves 6 to 8**

2 tablespoons (30 mL) extra-virgin olive oil

1 white onion, sliced

2½ pounds (1.125 kg) yellow beets, cubed (about 8 to 10 medium beets)

1 teaspoon (5 mL) turmeric

2 teaspoons (10 mL) salt, more to taste

2 tablespoons (30 mL) white vinegar

4 cups (1 L) low-sodium vegetable stock

Pinch of sugar (optional)

4 cups (1 L) shredded Napa cabbage

**To serve**

Full-fat sour cream

Chopped fresh dill

Caraway seeds

Hard boiled eggs, halved (optional)

I am a big fan of borscht any time of the year. This soup is so bright and beautiful, and it showcases how versatile beets and cabbage really are. Both vegetables can eat heavy, but here, in a turmeric-spiked vegetable stock finished with loads of dill, they are decidedly summery. This soup can be served hot or cold and also freezes really well.

In a Dutch oven over high heat, heat the olive oil. Once the oil begins to shimmer, add the onion, beets, turmeric, and salt. Stir to combine. Reduce the heat to medium and cover. Cook for 5 minutes, or until the onions soften and start to release some of their juices. Add the vinegar, vegetable stock, and sugar (if using). Increase the heat to high and cover. Once the soup starts to boil, reduce the heat to a simmer and cook for 20 to 25 minutes, until the beets are tender.

Carefully transfer about 2 cups (500 mL) of the cooked beets along with some of the stock to a high-speed blender. Purée until smooth. Return the puréed beets to the soup. Add the cabbage. Cook for 2 to 3 minutes, until the cabbage has wilted. Season with salt to taste.

**To serve:** Divide the soup among bowls. Top with sour cream, dill, caraway seeds, and hard boiled eggs (if using).

Store leftovers in an airtight container in the fridge for up to 4 days.

# Sauerkraut Soup

**Serves 6 to 8**

2 tablespoons (30 mL) unsalted butter

12 ounces (340 g) kielbasa, halved lengthwise and then sliced

1 onion, thinly sliced

1 medium turnip, cubed

¼ green cabbage, thinly sliced

4 cloves garlic, finely grated

1 tablespoon (15 mL) sweet paprika

1 tablespoon (15 mL) salt, more to taste

Pinch of sugar

1 jar (28 ounces/794 g) sauerkraut

1 can (28 ounces/794 g) whole peeled tomatoes, briefly crushed with your hands

4 cups (1 L) chicken stock

**To serve**

Rye bread

Unsalted butter

Flakey salt

Through a strange series of events in my very early twenties, I wound up enrolling in a university course on the aesthetics of Baroque opera. I had zero interest in opera, but the course took place in a small medieval town in Czech Republic and that was intriguing, so I signed up. The course was incredible (I now have an interest in Baroque opera!), but what I loved the most about that trip was the food. It was the first time I'd really eaten a distinct national cuisine and understood the context around it. Growing up in Canada and England, we might have eaten Italian one night and Indian the next, and I really had no concept that there was a history and culture connected to those cuisines, or that they were anything beyond "dinner." To travel to a place like Czech Republic and taste the dishes that had been made with regional ingredients for hundreds of years felt exciting and humbling all at the same time.

This soup was one of the first dishes I tried on that trip. Back in the tiny hostel kitchen, it was also the first dish I tried to replicate. It has gone through many iterations over the years. It is simple and hearty and, although not an exact replica, definitely a reasonable facsimile in keeping with the spirit of the original.

In a large Dutch oven over medium-high heat, melt the butter. Once it starts to bubble, add the kielbasa and cook, stirring occasionally, for 2 to 3 minutes, until it takes on a bit of colour. Add the onions and cook for 2 to 3 minutes, until they soften. Add the turnip, cabbage, garlic, paprika, salt, and sugar. Stir to combine. Add the sauerkraut (including the liquid), tomatoes, and stock. Cover and bring to a boil, then reduce the heat to a simmer. Let simmer for about 15 minutes, until the turnip is soft. Check the seasoning and add salt to taste.

**To serve:** Divide the soup among bowls. Slather some rye bread with butter, sprinkle it with flakey salt, and serve it on the side.

Store leftovers in an airtight container in the fridge for up to 5 days.

# Lentil Soup

**Serves 6 to 8**

2 tablespoons (30 mL) extra-virgin
    olive oil

2 medium carrots, diced

2 celery stalks, diced

1 medium yellow onion, diced

2 cloves garlic, finely grated or minced

2 teaspoons (10 mL) salt, more to taste

1 teaspoon (5 mL) ground cumin

1 teaspoon (5 mL) ground coriander

½ teaspoon (2 mL) turmeric

Pinch of cinnamon

1 red long chili, halved

1 cup (250 mL) split red lentils

1 can (28 ounces/794 g) whole peeled
    tomatoes, lightly crushed, plus
    ½ can water

4 cups (1 L) vegetable stock

**To serve**

Extra-virgin olive oil

Lemon wedges

Handful of fresh flat-leaf parsley,
    roughly chopped or torn

I am a huge fan of the author Laurie Colwin. She is most famous for her novels about New York society but also wrote two very cozy, very convivial books filled with essays and recipes that I like to read whenever I'm feeling uninspired about cooking. Laurie's writing makes all the ingredients seem approachable and even *friendly*. Like her, I also like to make delicious but not labour-intensive food. This is a very Laurie recipe, because lentil soup is nourishing and good and, as she says, "In all your life you will be hard-pressed to find something as simple, soothing, and forgiving, as consoling as lentil soup. You can take things out of it, or put things into it. It can be fancy or plain, and it will never let you down."

In a large Dutch oven over high heat, heat the olive oil until it shimmers. Add the carrots, celery, and onion. Cook, stirring occasionally, for about 5 minutes until softened slightly. Add the garlic, salt, cumin, coriander, turmeric, cinnamon, and chili. Cook for 1 minute. Add the lentils and stir to coat. Add the tomatoes, water, and stock. Bring to a boil, then reduce the heat to low. Stirring occasionally, simmer for 15 to 20 minutes, uncovered, until the lentils are tender. Season with salt to taste.

Ladle the soup into bowls and drizzle each serving with olive oil and a squeeze of lemon. Garnish with parsley.

Store leftovers in an airtight container in the fridge for up to 4 days.

# Brothy Farro with Mushrooms and Tofu

**Serves 4 to 6**

2 tablespoons (30 mL) extra-virgin olive oil

2 shallots, minced

1½ cups (375 mL) farro

2 teaspoons (10 mL) salt, more to taste

12 cups (3 L) low-sodium chicken or vegetable stock, warm

Small handful of fresh thyme sprigs, tied into a bundle

¼ pound (115 g) shiitake mushrooms, caps only, thinly sliced

1 pound (450 g) soft tofu, cubed or torn into chunks

Cracked black pepper

6 cups (1.5 L) baby spinach

Walnut oil, for drizzling

Early in my cooking career, I worked under a female head chef, which was an anomaly at the time. To this day I have no idea why, but we were all terrified of her. Rumours flew: She had worked at a fancy restaurant in Toronto! She was going to fire a lot of people! She ate her steak blue! To be fair, this all did end up being mostly true, but she also became one of the most inspiring chefs, both then and now, I know. Chef René introduced me to so many new ingredients and techniques and gave me a real education on creating flavour and composing dishes. This dish, a combination of farro, mushrooms, and tofu, is a riff on one of hers from almost 20 years ago. Like all good dishes (and good chefs), it has stood the test of time.

In a large heavy-bottomed saucepan or Dutch oven over medium-high heat, place the olive oil. Add the shallots and cook for 1 to 2 minutes, stirring so that they do not brown, until just barely translucent. Add the farro and toast it for 3 to 4 minutes until the colour deepens and it smells a bit nutty, stirring all the while so nothing burns. Add the salt, stir briefly, then add the warm stock and thyme. Stir to combine. Bring to a boil, cover, and reduce the heat to low. Let simmer for 20 minutes, until the farro is just starting to get tender. Remove the lid and continue simmering, uncovered, for another 10 to 15 minutes. Turn off the heat. Add the mushrooms, tofu, and spinach. Stir to combine. Cover and let sit for 5 minutes, until the mushrooms and tofu are warmed through and the spinach is wilted. Add salt and cracked black pepper to taste.

Ladle the stocky mixture into bowls and serve with a drizzle of walnut oil.

Store leftovers in an airtight container in the fridge for up to 3 days.

# Shakshuka with Chilies and Avocado

**Serves 4 to 6**

### Shakshuka

1 tablespoon (15 mL) extra-virgin olive oil

1 small yellow onion, grated or finely chopped

1 clove garlic, finely grated

1 teaspoon (5 mL) ground cumin

1 teaspoon (5 mL) ground coriander

1 teaspoon (5 mL) salt

Pinch of ground red chilies

1 can (28 ounces/794 g) whole peeled tomatoes, plus ½ can water

6 eggs

### To serve

3 radishes, chopped

1 to 2 green chilies, sliced

1 ear corn, kernels removed and cob discarded

1 avocado, pitted, peeled, and diced

½ cup (125 mL) cilantro, roughly chopped

1 lime

Corn tortillas, warm

Hot sauce

Lime wedges

Shakshuka is traditionally served in Israel at breakfast, but it makes such a wonderful and *quick* dinner as well. My daughters are always begging me for tacos, and this recipe is a mashup that incorporates shakshuka technique with Mexican flavours and can be made in as many minutes as it takes to chop an avocado and bake some eggs.

Preheat the oven to 400°F (200°C).

**Make the Shakshuka:** In a large cast iron skillet over high heat, heat the olive oil until shimmering. Add the onion and garlic. Cook for 2 to 3 minutes, stirring continuously, until the onions are softened and slightly translucent. Add the cumin, coriander, salt, and chilies. Cook for 1 minute, stirring all the while so the onions and garlic do not brown. Add the tomatoes and use a potato masher or wooden spoon to break them up a bit. Add the water and bring to a boil. Reduce the heat to low and simmer, uncovered, for about 10 minutes, until the sauce thickens.

Using a spoon, make a well in the sauce and gently crack an egg into it. Repeat 5 times. Carefully transfer the skillet to the oven for 8 to 10 minutes until the egg whites are set and the yolks are still creamy. Remove the shakshuka from the oven and let stand briefly while you prepare the other ingredients.

**To serve:** Sprinkle the hot shakshuka with the radishes, chilies, corn, avocado, and cilantro. Juice the lime overtop. Serve immediately with warm tortillas for dipping, hot sauce, and lime wedges.

**Tip:** *If you want a little more texture or you're catering to a younger crowd, you can serve this over corn chips or even (!) Fritos. I would be lying if I said I have never dipped a Cool Ranch Dorito in my shakshuka. Feel free to colour outside the lines and get creative.*

# Jammy Tomatoes and Butter Bean Bake

**Serves 4**

4 vine or Roma tomatoes, chopped

2 cups (500 mL) grape tomatoes, halved

1 jar (10 ounces/296 mL) roasted bell peppers, strained and chopped

½ loaf stale bread, torn into chunks

1 shallot, thinly sliced

2 cloves garlic, thinly sliced

1 celery heart, thinly sliced, leaves set aside

2 tablespoons (30 mL) extra-virgin olive oil, more for drizzling

2 teaspoons (10 mL) sherry vinegar

Salt and cracked black pepper, to taste

Pinch of granulated sugar (optional)

4 ounces (115 g) Macedonian feta, broken into bite-size chunks

1 can (14 ounces/400 mL) butter beans, drained and rinsed

A new recipe can come from the right ingredients, the right inspiration, or even the right idea. This recipe came from the wrong idea. As I was paging through Paul Kahan's *Cooking for Good Times*, I saw the most stunning tomato bake thing, and I immediately wanted to re-create it. It had all sorts of squishy roasted tomatoes, golden toasted bread chunks, and glistening butter beans. I closed the book and turned my attention to something else (probably a toddler or a load of laundry), but I kept thinking about the dish and how I would make it. I went back to the book a couple of days later to check the recipe. There was no recipe, in fact—or at least not the one I was looking for—because the picture I had been looking at was a collection of ingredients to be puréed into a sauce (it was romesco, and the beans were Marcona almonds). I was not derailed and went ahead as planned with the recipe I had imagined. It was delicious, and so here it is. Maybe someday Paul Kahan, or even you, dear reader, will glance briefly at the photo opposite and be inspired to make a totally amazing soup.

Preheat the oven to 425°F (220°C). Line a rimmed baking sheet with parchment paper.

In a medium bowl, place the vine and grape tomatoes, peppers, bread, shallot, garlic, and celery heart. Add the olive oil, vinegar, salt and pepper, and sugar (if using). Toss to combine. Let marinate for 15 to 20 minutes, stirring occasionally to distribute juices.

Spread the vegetable mixture out on the prepared baking sheet. Bake for 10 to 15 minutes, until the vine tomatoes have softened and the grape tomatoes have gone jammy. Scatter the feta evenly overtop and switch the oven to broil. Broil for 3 to 5 minutes, until the cheese has softened. Let cool for 2 to 3 minutes. Top with the butter beans, celery leaves, and another drizzle of olive oil. Serve immediately.

Store leftovers in an airtight container in the fridge for up to 4 days.

# Roasted Butternut Squash with Labneh and Pistachios

**Serves 4**

1 small butternut squash, cut into
   3-inch (8 cm) chunks

2 tablespoons (30 mL) extra-virgin
   olive oil

1 teaspoon (5 mL) kosher salt

1 teaspoon (5 mL) ground coriander

½ teaspoon (2 mL) ground red chilies

1 teaspoon (5 mL) sweet paprika

1 cup (250 mL) labneh

Zest and juice of 1 lime

2 tablespoons (30 mL) Pickled Chilies
   (page 291), plus a splash of brine

¼ cup (60 mL) pistachios, toasted and
   chopped (see Toasted Nuts, page 290)

Large handful of mint, roughly chopped

Squash can easily become overpoweringly sweet, which is why I like to pair it with spice. Here, it gets covered in coriander, chilies, and paprika before being roasted. Then it gets plunked in a pool of creamy labneh and covered in crunchy pistachios, fresh mint, bright lime, and fiery pickled chilies. This is hands down my favourite way to eat squash. Even though there's a lot going on, it all works. Serve this dish warm, at ambient temperature, or chilled—it is always delicious.

Preheat the oven to 475°F (240°C). Line a rimmed baking sheet with parchment paper.

Place the squash in a medium bowl. Add the olive oil, salt, coriander, chilies, and paprika. Toss to combine.

Spread out the squash on the prepared baking sheet. Roast for 18 to 20 minutes, until slightly charred and easily pierced with a paring knife.

Spread the labneh over a large plate or platter. Mound the squash on top. Top with the lime zest and juice, pickled chilies and brine, pistachios, and mint. Serve warm, at room temperature, or cold. If you're prepping in advance, cover the platter and keep it in the fridge until ready to serve.

Store leftovers in an airtight container in the fridge for up to 4 days.

# Roasted Delicata Squash and Feta with Hot Honey

**Serves 4**

2 medium delicata squash, halved
  and seeded

1 small red onion, thinly sliced

2 tablespoons (30 mL) extra-virgin
  olive oil, more for drizzling

1 tablespoon (15 mL) apple cider vinegar

1 teaspoon (5 mL) salt

Pinch of ground red chilies

8 ounces (225 g) Greek feta

2 tablespoons (30 mL) Hot Honey
  (page 293), more for the table

Juice of ½ lemon

Charred bread, to serve

I love delicata squash, but it's definitely not as common as butternut or spaghetti squash, and I think we should change that. Delicata squash has all the roastability I'm looking for in a gourd but doesn't taste too *squash-y*. It's also easy to prep, since the peel is edible and you don't have to remove it. However, if the skin looks thick, I usually grab my Y peeler (page 17) and remove a little of the skin regardless, as it can be tough. Because the flavour of delicata squash is more subtle than that of other squash, I don't like to do too much to it—just give it a little ride in the oven with extra-virgin olive oil, acid, and spice. This dish is great alongside a bright green salad with loads of herbs and maybe a store-bought rotisserie chicken, but it's also great smashed onto a big hunk of charred bread and dunked into some Warm Chorizo in Sidra (page 38) or layered under some Prosciutto Wrapped Eggplant (page 142).

Preheat the oven to 475°F (240°C). Line a rimmed baking sheet with parchment paper.

Place the squash and onion in a large bowl. Drizzle with the olive oil, the vinegar, salt, and chilies. Spread the vegetables out on the prepared baking sheet. Cube or crumble the feta into large chunks and sprinkle evenly overtop.

Bake for 15 to 20 minutes, until the squash is slightly charred and fork tender. Remove from the oven and transfer everything (including any juices) to a large plate.

Drizzle the squash with the hot honey and top with the lemon juice and additional olive oil. Serve immediately alongside the charred bread and extra hot honey.

Store leftovers in an airtight container in the fridge for up to 4 days.

# Prosciutto Wrapped Eggplant

**Serves 4**

4 cups (1 L) lukewarm water

2 tablespoons (30 mL) salt

2 medium eggplants, sliced lengthwise
¾ inch (2 cm) thick

8 slices prosciutto

2 tablespoons (30 mL) neutral oil,
such as grapeseed or canola,
for frying

This is a very simple dish that looks best when everything is a little imperfect and no two eggplant pieces are alike. There's a haphazard sophistication to the crispy snarls of prosciutto wrapped around the eggplant. Fried to perfection, the eggplant inside is tender and even a bit creamy. This dish requires only a few ingredients and no fancy techniques, but it never fails to impress, and it always disappears quickly. Should you be lucky enough to have leftovers, or smart enough to double the recipe, I can confirm that leftover PWE tucked into a warm pita or a wedge of bread, slathered with Tahini Dip (page 294), and topped with a handful of arugula and perhaps some roasted red peppers from a jar is basically heaven on earth.

In a medium bowl, whisk the water and salt until the salt dissolves. Drop the eggplant into the mixture and let brine for 20 minutes. Remove the eggplant from the brine and shake off the excess moisture. Pat the eggplant pieces dry with paper towels. Wrap each piece in a slice of prosciutto.

In a heavy skillet over medium-high heat, heat the oil. Once the oil starts to shimmer, add a few slices of prosciutto wrapped eggplant, being careful not to crowd the pan. Fry until the prosciutto is crispy and the eggplant has charred slightly, about 4 to 5 minutes on each side. Transfer the eggplant to a clean plate. Repeat until all of the eggplant has been fried. Serve immediately.

Store leftovers in an airtight container in the fridge for up to 4 days.

# Crispy Eggplant with Spicy Vinaigrette

**Serves 4 to 6**

To me, this dish is perfect. It features fried eggplant, a spicy Aleppo-spiked vinaigrette, a creamy pool of feta, and then loads of nutty herbs on top. There is nothing else I could want, except maybe some warm pita and the company of other people who like to eat with their hands.

### Eggplant

4 cups (1 L) lukewarm water

2 tablespoons (30 mL) salt, more for finishing

2 to 3 medium eggplants, sliced into ¾-inch (2 cm) rounds

1 cup (250 mL) neutral oil, such as grapeseed or canola, for frying

### Vinaigrette

¼ cup (60 mL) extra-virgin olive oil

2 cloves garlic, smashed

1 teaspoon (5 mL) cumin seeds

Pinch of sugar (optional)

Juice of 1 lemon

1 teaspoon (5 mL) Aleppo pepper

1 teaspoon (5 mL) sweet paprika

Pinch of salt

### To serve

1 cup (250 mL) Feta Cream (page 294)

¼ cup (60 mL) pistachios, toasted and chopped (see Toasted Nuts, page 290)

1 green bird's eye chili, sliced

½ cup (125 mL) fresh flat-leaf parsley, roughly chopped or torn

½ cup (125 mL) fresh mint, roughly chopped or torn

**Fry the Eggplant:** In a medium bowl, whisk together the water and salt until the salt dissolves. Drop in the eggplant and let brine for 20 minutes. Remove the eggplant from the brine and shake off the excess moisture. Pat the eggplant dry with paper towels.

Line a plate with paper towels. In a large heavy-bottomed skillet over medium-high heat, heat about one quarter of the oil. Once the oil starts to shimmer, add a few slices of eggplant, being careful not to crowd the pan. Fry until the eggplant has charred slightly, about 4 to 5 minutes on each side. Transfer the eggplant to the prepared plate and season with a pinch of salt. Repeat to fry the remaining eggplant in batches, adding more oil to the skillet as necessary and seasoning the finished slices.

**Make the Vinaigrette:** Discard any oil remaining in the skillet and wipe it out with a paper towel. Place the olive oil, garlic, and cumin in the skillet and cook over high heat, just until the cumin becomes aromatic, about 2 to 3 minutes. Remove the skillet from the heat. Slowly stir in the sugar (if using) and lemon juice. Add the Aleppo, paprika, and salt. Whisk to combine.

**To serve:** Dollop the feta cream in the centre of a large plate. Using a spoon, push the cream from the centre of the plate to its edges. Place the fried eggplant rounds on top of the feta cream. Spoon the warm vinaigrette over the eggplant. Sprinkle with the pistachios, chili, parsley, and mint. Serve immediately.

Store leftovers in an airtight container in the fridge for up to 4 days.

# Alone in the Kitchen
# with a Cabbage

I don't just have an affinity for cabbage. I also feel a kinship with the lumpy, rather plebeian cruciferous vegetable. You might not pick either one of us as being special from across the room (or produce aisle), but given the right treatment—and maybe a thoughtful garnish, darn it—we are capable not necessarily of being transformed but of letting the things that make us so very cabbage-y in the first place shine. (The longevity! The layers! The substance! The downright nuttiness!) In that moment, we can be compelling.

As a young person, I did not fully respect the appeal of cabbage because the way cabbage was typically prepared in my house was not appealing. I don't want to throw shade at anyone's cooking, but cabbage was either red and boiled with apple slices (please note that I am hot fruit averse, so this did skew the experience) or green and shredded alongside thin strips of carrot and a handful of raisins (I am also dried-fruit-in-salads averse) in some form of coleslaw. It wasn't until I had my daughters that I began to see all the potential wrapped up in a cabbage. With two toddlers, running to the grocery store daily on a whim became not just implausible but impossible. There's so much less *whimming* when you have children, and so my relationship with cabbage became more meaningful as I came to rely on having a vegetable in the fridge that could last days and even, at times, weeks to provide easy nourishment and an *option* of something to cook.

I started to appreciate having one or two cabbages around because they offer—in a very economical way, mind you—a springboard for culinary creativity. There are, in fact, many substantive cabbage-centric dishes that pull in a few other ingredients and can form the centre of a meal. Fried Cabbage with Halloumi and Jalapenos (page 151) is bright, a little spicy, and crunchy-cheesy and hits all the right notes for me, especially in warmer months. Sauerkraut Soup (page 129) and Braised Red Cabbage with Cider and Bacon (page 85) are a bit more classic, but they are simple in their ingredient lists and warming and rely on everyday pantry items to put together. Spicy Oven Charred Cabbage and Lemons (page 152) has become a favourite in our household because it is a snap to assemble and chuck in the oven. It also goes so well with Hot Honey Roast Chicken (page 210) and

Celery with Walnuts, Feta, and Dill (page 62), and you can buy some store-bought pita or naan and get an absolutely mouthwatering meal on the table in about a half an hour. Hominy Cab 'n' Cheese (page 98) is kid friendly and has just enough béchamel and bread crumbs to convert even grown-up cabbage skeptics. Cabbage can also bulk out a dish or be swapped in for heartier greens—add about 1 cup (250 mL) or more to the skillet when you cook the onions for the Tartiflette (page 102) or use it in place of kale in Mapo Tofu with Greens (page 224).

For a quick slaw or condiment to put out, perhaps beside Cod and Zucchini in Curry Coconut Broth (page 195) or even Herb Stuffed Rainbow Trout (page 200), thinly slice about a quarter of a green, red, napa, or pointed cabbage and place it in a medium bowl. Sprinkle liberally with kosher salt and then about 1 to 2 teaspoons (5 to 10 mL) granulated sugar or honey. Using your hands, massage well so that the cabbage softens and releases some of its crunch. Drizzle with olive or canola oil and then 1 tablespoon (15 mL) or so of white or apple cider vinegar (or any vinegar, really). Toss briefly and serve as you like.

Given the breadth of my cabbage repertoire, you won't be surprised to hear that one of the greatest compliments I've received about my cooking made direct reference to the vegetable. Once, after a couple of years of shared meals, a roommate turned to me and said, "You know, even when we don't live together, I'm still going to eat a lot of cabbage." It could be that this was more about the cabbage than it was about my culinary skills, but perhaps it was about both. I like to think that what I bring to cabbage is a sense of possibility. For me, that means something—that something very regular and at times overlooked can become something both useful and special.

# Fried Cabbage with Halloumi and Jalapenos

**Serves 4 to 6**

3 tablespoons (45 mL) neutral oil, such as canola or grapeseed, divided

½ cabbage, cored and chopped

Salt and cracked black pepper

2 cloves garlic, finely grated

Juice of 1 lemon, divided

1 pound (450 g) halloumi, cut into ½-inch (1 cm) slices

1 tablespoon (15 mL) Hot Honey (page 293)

1 jalapeno, thinly sliced

2 tablespoons (30 mL) toasted pine nuts (see Toasted Nuts, page 290)

¼ cup (60 mL) fresh cilantro, chopped

¼ cup (60 mL) fresh basil, chopped

It's no secret that I always have a green cabbage on hand. This is one of those recipes that just sort of *happened* on a Tuesday night when I was staring at a series of odds and ends in the fridge with hungry toddlers clamouring in the background. There's almost zero prep, and the whole thing comes together quickly, but because of all the good sweet, salty, spicy, herby crunchiness, it's the kind of dish that hits all the right notes and disappears quickly.

In a large skillet over high heat, heat 2 tablespoons (30 mL) of the oil until shimmering. Add the cabbage and season with salt and pepper. Cook, without stirring, for about 5 minutes, until the cabbage begins to caramelize and soften. Add the garlic and reduce the heat to medium. Cover and cook for another 5 minutes or so, until the cabbage loses its crunch but still has some texture. Add more salt and pepper to taste and squeeze the juice of ½ lemon overtop. Stir to combine. Transfer the cabbage to a large platter.

Line a plate with paper towels. Wipe out the skillet (no need to be too particular). Add the remaining 1 tablespoon (15 mL) oil to the skillet and place it over medium-high heat. Once the oil begins to shimmer, gently fry the halloumi on both sides, about 2 to 3 minutes per side. Using a perforated spatula, transfer the halloumi to the prepared plate. Let drain for 1 minute. Arrange the halloumi on top of the cabbage.

Squeeze juice from the remaining ½ lemon over the cabbage and halloumi. Drizzle with the hot honey. Top with the jalapenos, pine nuts, cilantro, and basil. Serve immediately.

Store leftovers in an airtight container in the refrigerator for up to 5 days.

# Spicy Oven Charred Cabbage and Lemons

**Serves 4 to 6**

### Pita Chips

1 pita, torn into bite-size pieces

1 tablespoon (15 mL) neutral oil, such as canola or grapeseed

Pinch of salt

Pinch of Aleppo pepper

### Cabbage

½ medium green cabbage, cored

½ cup (125 mL) neutral oil, such as canola or grapeseed, divided

4 cloves Garlic Confit (page 286)

1 lemon, thinly sliced and seeded

1 red bird's eye chili, halved

½ teaspoon (2 mL) salt

4 ounces (115 g) feta cheese (Macedonian, if you can get it)

¼ cup (60 mL) Harissa (page 296)

¼ cup (60 mL) fresh flat-leaf parsley, chopped

¼ cup (60 mL) fresh mint, chopped

Juice of ½ lemon

To my knowledge, this is an original recipe born out of a "what shall we eat for dinner tonight?" situation. I didn't have many ingredients in the fridge and, as I recall, they all ended up in the recipe. Don't be misled by this dish's origin story. It is *so good*. The lemon gets a bit charred and chewy, the cabbage is nutty and coated in spicy, garnet-coloured harissa, and the herbs and crispy pita add just the perfect amount of aromatic crunch to cut through the heat. I love eating this dish alongside a Hot Honey Roast Chicken (page 210) or with a dish of hummus, a can of stuffed grape leaves, and Turkish bread.

**Make the Pita Chips:** Preheat the oven to 425°F (220°C). Line a rimmed baking sheet with parchment paper.

In a small bowl, toss the pita with the oil, salt, and Aleppo. Spread the pita in a single layer on the prepared baking sheet. Bake for 5 to 6 minutes, until crispy and brown. Set aside. Increase the oven temperature to 500°F (260°C).

**Make the Cabbage:** With the flat side of the cabbage down, cut it into quarters. Cut each quarter in half on a slight angle so that you end up with 8 pieces. Don't be too fussy about this, as the cabbage will break up more as it cooks. Drizzle about 2 tablespoons (30 mL) of the oil into a large cast iron skillet. Nestle in the cabbage, followed by the garlic confit, lemon, and chili. Drizzle the remaining oil over top. Season with the salt.

Roast the cabbage for 20 to 30 minutes, giving it a gentle stir occasionally to make sure it doesn't stick. When it's crispy and brown, remove it from the oven and crumble the feta overtop. Return the cabbage to the oven for another 3 to 5 minutes until the feta gets a bit melty. Remove from the oven and dollop the harissa on top.

Sprinkle the pita chips on the hot cabbage. Top with the parsley, mint, and lemon juice. Serve immediately.

Store leftovers in an airtight container in the refrigerator for up to 4 days.

# Celeriac à la Meunière

**Serves 4 to 6**

2 medium heads of celeriac

¼ cup (60 mL) extra-virgin olive oil

1 teaspoon (5 mL) salt

2 lemons

8 tablespoons (115 g) butter, cubed

2 tablespoons (30 mL) capers, plus
   a splash of their juice

¼ cup (60 mL) Dukkah (page 297)

½ cup (125 mL) fresh flat-leaf parsley

It turns out that celeriac that's been poked with a fork many times, smothered in olive oil and salt, and roasted until it's more or less caramelized is basically the most delicious thing ever. When you make a brown butter caper sauce to go with it, well, you should probably plan on wearing elastic-waist pants under your apron. You can make this dish any time, but it really shines when you invite over a vegetarian friend who is used to being served a token grain salad or perhaps a microwaved veggie burger as a default vegetarian option. They will think you are the most amazing cook because you will have made something vegetarian that tastes so good, and you will have no choice but to agree with them.

Preheat the oven to 475°F (240°C). Line a rimmed baking sheet with parchment paper.

Place the whole celeriac heads on the prepared baking sheet. Using a fork, poke each celeriac about 20 times all over. Drizzle each head evenly with the olive oil and sprinkle with the salt. Rub the oil and salt into the celeriac.

Roast for 30 to 40 minutes, basting occasionally, until the celeriac heads are golden brown, easily pierced with a paring knife, and oozing their own celeriac caramel. Let stand until the celeriac is cool enough to handle. Keep the oven on.

Using a sharp paring knife, trim the ends off each lemon. Stand one lemon on end. Starting at the top, slide your knife downward between the flesh of the lemon and the pith so that you cut away the peel in a 1- to 1½-inch (2.5 to 4 cm) strip. Repeat, working your knife around the lemon so that only the flesh remains and any white pith has been removed. Repeat with the second lemon. Discard the peel.

*recipe continues*

Working over a small bowl to catch the juice, hold the lemon firmly in your non-dominant hand. Use the paring knife to segment the lemon: carefully slice into the centre of the lemon alongside the membrane. Twist your knife, work your way back up the other side of the lemon segment, and pop it out so you have a wedge of lemon and no membrane. Put the lemon wedge into the small bowl with any juice you have collected and repeat this step, carefully, until you have separated all the lemon segments from both lemons. Squeeze any juice in the remaining membrane into the bowl and discard the membrane.

In a medium skillet over medium-high heat, melt the butter. Keep an eye on it as it starts to bubble but continue cooking until the milk solids toast and become brown and the butter starts to smell nutty. Add the capers and let them fry in the butter briefly, about 1 minute. Turn off the heat. Immediately add the caper juice and lemon segments and their juice, and stir to combine. Set aside while you finish the celeriac.

Preheat the oven to broil. Place an oven rack on the second slot from the top.

Place the celeriac on a cutting board and slice it into rounds about 1 to 1½ inches (2.5 to 4 cm) thick. Return the celeriac to the same baking sheet you used to roast it, laying the slices in a single layer so that they can get a bit of a tan under the broiler. Broil for 4 to 5 minutes, until they are charred but not burnt.

Transfer the celeriac to a platter and spoon the brown butter caper sauce over top. Garnish with the dukkah and parsley. Serve immediately.

Store leftovers in an airtight container in the fridge for up to 4 days.

# Roasted Beet and Socca Tart

**Serves 4**

4 to 5 medium beets

2 tablespoons (30 mL) walnut oil, divided, more for drizzling

Juice of ½ lemon

Cracked black pepper

1 cup (250 mL) minus 1 tablespoon (15 mL) chickpea flour

1 cup (250 mL) water

1 teaspoon (5 mL) salt, more for seasoning

1 cup (250 mL) Feta Cream (page 294) or skyr

½ cup (125 mL) thinly sliced fennel

½ cup (125 mL) baby arugula

¼ cup (60 mL) toasted walnuts, chopped

Socca flour is made from chickpeas and has a slightly nutty flavour. It's inexpensive and high in protein. It's also extremely easy to make a crust from, so for this earthy tart topped with beets and feta, it forms the crust. It's great to serve to a crowd because it's so simple and also happens to be gluten free. If you want to make it vegan, you can swap out the Feta Cream (page 294) for an equal amount of Tahini Dip (page 294) or Pistachio Butter (page 231). And if you don't happen to have beets, you can easily substitute roasted carrots, squash, or even tomatoes. If you don't have time for toppings at all, just serve the socca on its own. Simply cut it into wedges and drizzle it with a little olive oil. When you place it next to an aperitivo and a dish of warm olive oil–fried almonds, you and your guests will suddenly feel very hip and European.

Preheat the oven to 475°F (240°C).

If your beets come with tops, cut them off and reserve for another use. Place the beets on a rimmed baking sheet. Roast for 40 to 50 minutes, until easily pierced with a paring knife. Set aside to cool.

When the beets are cool enough to handle, use a paring knife to peel them. Cut the beets into bite-size chunks. Drizzle with 1 tablespoon (15 mL) of the walnut oil and the lemon juice. Season with salt and pepper to taste. Toss to combine.

Meanwhile, in a medium bowl, whisk together the chickpea flour, water, the remaining 1 tablespoon (15 mL) walnut oil, and the salt. Cover and let stand at room temperature for at least 1 hour. If you're going to let it stand for more than 2 hours, transfer it to the fridge where it can stay, covered, overnight.

Preheat the oven to 500°F (260°C). Lightly grease an 11-inch (28 cm) ovenproof skillet and place in the hot oven to heat up.

*recipe continues*

When the oven and the pan are both hot, use a thick oven mitt to remove the skillet from the oven. Give the socca batter a final mix and then pour it into the hot pan. Return the skillet back to the oven and cook the socca until golden brown, about 12 to 15 minutes. Turn on the broiler for 1 to 2 minutes to give the top of the socca just a kiss of char. Remove from the oven and let cool slightly.

Generously spread the warm (but not hot) socca tart with the feta cream. Top evenly with the beets, fennel, arugula, and walnuts. Drizzle with a little more walnut oil. Serve immediately.

Store leftovers in an airtight container in the fridge for up to 2 days.

# Half-Cooked Tomato Sauce with Hand Cut Pasta

**Serves 2 to 4**

A raw tomato and a cooked tomato are two very different things. When I have a handmade pasta party, I want to invite them both. This dish is best served at the peak of summer, when the garden is overflowing with all sorts of tomatoes. Tie on an apron and pour yourself an icy glass of Chablis while you make the pasta or recruit your children to do the kneading. There are a lot of steps, but don't let that put you off this recipe. It doesn't require a ton of effort, just tomatoes.

### Sauce

3 to 4 vine-ripened or heirloom tomatoes, chopped

1 pint (500 mL) mixed cherry tomatoes, halved

¼ cup (60 mL) extra-virgin olive oil

3 cloves garlic, smashed

½ teaspoon (2 mL) salt

Pinch of sugar (optional)

### Pasta

2½ cups (625 mL) 00 flour, more for dusting

4 large eggs

2 large egg yolks

1 to 2 tablespoons (15 to 30 mL) water

1 tablespoon (15 mL) extra-virgin olive oil

1 teaspoon (5 mL) salt

### To serve

Extra-virgin olive oil, for drizzling

½ cup (125 mL) fresh basil, roughly chopped or torn

2 ounces (55 g) pecorino cheese, more for garnish

**Tip:** *This recipe calls for 00 flour, which is available at most grocery stores and is just super finely ground all-purpose flour. If you can't find it, the same amount of regular old all-purpose flour works too.*

**Start the Sauce:** In a medium bowl, place the vine-ripened and cherry tomatoes, olive oil, garlic, salt, and sugar (if using). Stir to combine. Let sit at room temperature for at least 1 hour but no more than 3 hours. If you think of it, stir the sauce ingredients a few times as they sit.

**Make the Pasta Dough:** On a large clean work surface, place the flour in a neat pile. Using your hands, make a well in the flour. In a small bowl, whisk together the eggs, egg yolks, 1 tablespoon (15 mL) of the water, the olive oil, and salt. Pour the mixture into the well. Using a fork, mix the egg mixture outwards into the flour, and as you begin to make a dough, use a dough knife to help you scrape the flour up into a dough ball. If the dough feels a bit shaggy, add the remaining water. Once it comes together, knead the dough with your hands for about 10 minutes, sprinkling in a little additional flour if the dough starts to stick to the work surface. Form the dough into a ball and cover it tightly in plastic wrap. Let rest at room temperature for 20 minutes.

**Half-Cook the Sauce:** Heat a large skillet or Dutch oven over high heat. Scoop the garlic out of the tomato sauce and discard. Use a perforated spoon to hold back about half the tomatoes and tip the other half of the tomatoes and most of the juice into the hot skillet. Cook for 4 to 5 minutes, until the tomatoes get a bit jammy and most of the liquid has cooked down. Reduce the heat to low and let it bubble slowly while the pasta is cooked.

**Finish the Pasta:** Bring a saucepan of salted water to a rolling boil. Cover and reduce the heat to a simmer so

*recipe continues*

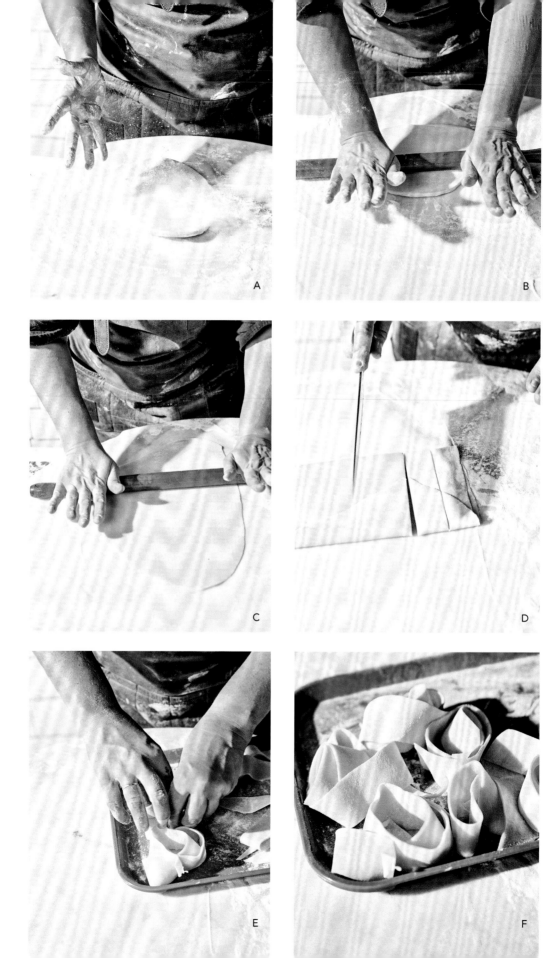

that the water is ready when it's time to cook the pasta.

Using a dough knife, cut the dough into quarters. Flour your counter well and place one piece of dough in front of you. Using a large rolling pin, roll the portion of dough into a long strip. Continue to sprinkle the dough with just enough flour to keep it from sticking to the counter and the rolling pin. Lift the dough up and off the counter after each roll to ensure that it remains free moving. Continue rolling until the dough is about ⅛ inch (3 mm) thick—as thin as possible without it tearing or breaking when you lift it.

Place the rectangle of dough on your work surface so that one of the short ends is closest to your body. Fold the bottom quarter of the dough up, then fold it up three more times over itself to make a large flat jelly roll of pasta. Using a sharp knife, cut the pasta into strips about 1½-inches (4 cm) wide. Unroll each strip of pasta and then reroll it loosely into a nest so that air can circulate around the noodles. Dust each nest with a little more flour to coat if the pasta is sticking together. Place the noodle nests neatly on a rimmed baking sheet. Repeat the steps above to roll out and cut the remaining 3 portions of dough.

Increase the heat under the pasta water to high and bring it to a rolling boil. Working in batches of about 3 or 4 nests at a time, so that the pasta water stays at a rolling boil, cook the pasta for 1 to 2 minutes, until it's *just* cooked. Using tongs or a perforated ladle, transfer the cooked pasta to the bowl of raw tomato sauce. Once all the pasta has been cooked and tossed into the raw tomato sauce, tip the entire bowl into the skillet of cooked sauce and increase the heat under the skillet to high. Cook over high heat, stirring so that everything mixes nicely, for about 1 minute until the pasta and raw tomatoes are warmed through. Drizzle with olive oil and add the basil. Toss to combine.

Grate the pecorino overtop. Serve immediately.

Store leftovers in an airtight container in the fridge for up to 2 days.

# Pumpkin Stuffed Shells with Brown Butter Béchamel

**Serves 4 to 6**

½ pound (225 g) large shell pasta

### Filling

1 small sugar pumpkin
1 tablespoon (15 mL) extra-virgin olive oil
Pinch of salt
6 cups (1.5 L) raw spinach, roughly
   chopped
8 ounces (225 g) mascarpone cheese
2 egg yolks, beaten
Pinch of ground nutmeg
Pinch of ground red chilies
Salt and cracked black pepper
¼ cup (60 mL) Bread Crumbs (page 289)

### Sauce

2 tablespoons (30 mL) unsalted butter
2 tablespoons (30 mL) all-purpose flour
2 cups (500 mL) 2% milk, warm
2 ounces (55 g) Mimolette or aged
   Gouda cheese, grated
Salt and cracked black pepper

Stuffed shells are having a bit of a moment, and why shouldn't they? Hot, creamy, cheesy pasta, bursting with more hot, creamy, cheesy filling holds universal appeal. Although the usual stuffed shell suspects are here (pasta, mascarpone cheese, spinach), I bring in some fall flavours. After all, the ideal stuffed shell experience involves wearing a sweater and some really cozy wool socks, and you just can't do that in August. Roasted pumpkin, brown butter, and nutty Mimolette cheese all add a bit of interest to these stuffed shells. Stuffing the shells can be a bit fiddly, so I recommend you put on an apron over your lovely sweater, turn up the music, and get lost in making something delicious on a cool day.

Bring a large saucepan of salted water to a rolling boil. Add the shells and cook to al dente according to package instructions, making sure to stir occasionally so the shells don't stick to each other or the bottom of the pot. Drain. Spread the shells out on a clean baking sheet to cool.

Preheat the oven to 475°F (240°C). Line a large rimmed baking sheet with parchment paper.

**Make the Filling:** Cut the sugar pumpkin in half and scoop out the seeds. Brush the cut side of each pumpkin half with the oil and sprinkle with a pinch of salt. Place the pumpkin halves, cut side down, on the prepared baking sheet. Roast for 20 to 30 minutes, until the skin is easily pierced with a paring knife. Flip the pumpkin halves so that the skin side is down. Set aside until the pumpkin is cool enough to handle. Reduce the oven temperature to 400°F (200°C).

**Stuff the shells:** Using a large spoon, scoop the warm pumpkin flesh out of its skin and into a medium bowl. You should end up with about 3 cups (750 mL) of flesh, and it should be soft enough that you can break it up with the spoon. Add the spinach and stir so that the spinach wilts. Add the mascarpone, egg yolks, nutmeg, and chilies. Stir to combine. Season with salt and pepper to taste.

*recipe continues*

Using a spoon, load the filling into the shells. Don't get too fussy with it but enjoy the meditative opportunity this task affords. Place the filled shells into a 13- × 9-inch (3.5 L) baking dish so that they're just touching.

**Make the Sauce:** In a large heavy-bottomed saucepan or Dutch oven over medium-high heat, melt the butter until it just starts to froth and bubble. Sprinkle in the flour and whisk vigorously to ensure that there are no lumps. Whisking continuously, cook the butter and flour mixture (it's called a roux now) for 2 to 3 minutes, making sure it does not brown, until a thick paste forms. Slowly whisk in the warm milk and continue cooking and stirring until the sauce becomes thick and creamy, about 5 to 7 minutes. Remove the saucepan from the heat. Add the cheese and stir until melted. Season with salt and pepper to taste.

Pour the sauce over the prepared shells and top with the bread crumbs. Bake for 20 to 25 minutes, until the sauce is bubbling. Serve immediately.

Store leftovers in an airtight container in the fridge for up to 4 days.

# Green Lasagna

## Serves 6 to 8

1 box (16 ounces/450 g) lasagna noodles
Extra-virgin olive oil, for brushing

### Filling
2 pounds (900 g) green zucchini, grated
1 tablespoon (15 mL) salt, more to taste
Pinch of ground red chilies
1 small jar (6 ounces/170 g) herb pesto

### Sauce
6 tablespoons (85 g) unsalted butter
6 tablespoons (90 mL) all-purpose flour
5 cups (1.25 L) whole milk (3.25%), warm
Pinch of nutmeg
2 cups (500 mL) grated pecorino cheese
2 cups (500 mL) grated mozzarella
   cheese

My sister-in-law, Donna, is half Italian and has a lot of strong feelings about food and noodles, specifically. It has not been a difficult adjustment for me to get used to there being a pasta dish at every family dinner. It's Christmas? Sure, pass me the penne with Bolognese sauce. Easter? How about some fresh cavatelli? Birthday? Cannelloni, of course! This mouthwatering, zucchini and pesto–loaded lasagna was a "side dish" at Thanksgiving a few years back, and as someone who has never really been a huge turkey fan, it took up a good deal of real estate on my plate. I'd never had a non-tomato-based lasagna before, but I was hooked. (Will you judge me if I tell you I had never even considered such a thing was possible?) Donna kindly parted with the recipe, which is actually from Italy and requires a lot of steps, including rolling your own pasta. If you are the sort of person who enjoys rolling your own pasta, you absolutely can, and you will probably enjoy it. Rolling out pasta is a task I only *sometimes* enjoy, so I opt to use boxed pasta here.

Bring a large saucepan of salted water to a rolling boil. Add the noodles and cook to al dente according to package instructions, making sure to stir occasionally so the noodles don't stick to each other or the bottom of the pot. Drain. Set the noodles on a clean baking sheet, brushing both sides with a little olive oil to keep them from drying out and sticking together. If you need to stack the noodles on top of each other, place a piece of parchment paper between the layers.

**Prepare the Filling:** Line a fine-mesh sieve or colander with cheesecloth or a clean kitchen towel. Place the zucchini in the cheesecloth and sprinkle it with the salt. Using your hands, toss the zucchini. Set aside to drain while you prepare the sauce.

*recipe continues*

**Make the Sauce:** In a large heavy-bottomed saucepan or Dutch oven over medium-high heat, melt the butter until it just starts to froth and bubble. Sprinkle in the flour and whisk vigorously to ensure that there are no lumps. Whisking continuously, cook the butter and flour mixture (it's called a roux now) for 2 to 3 minutes, making sure it does not brown, until a thick paste forms. Slowly whisk in the warm milk and continue cooking and stirring until the sauce becomes thick and creamy, about 5 to 7 minutes. Remove the saucepan from the heat. Add the nutmeg, pecorino, and mozzarella. Stir until the cheese melts.

Preheat the oven to 350°F (180°C).

**Finish the Filling and Assemble the Lasagna:** Using your hands, give the zucchini a good squeeze to remove any excess moisture. Transfer it to a medium bowl, add the chilies and pesto, and toss. It should be plenty seasoned but check the taste; if it needs another pinch of salt, go for it.

Spoon about ¼ cup (60 mL) of the sauce into the bottom of a 13- × 9-inch (3.5 L) baking dish. Arrange a layer of noodles in the bottom of the dish, trimming to fit where required. Spread about one third of the zucchini mixture over the noodles. Top with about one quarter of the remaining sauce and then another layer of noodles. Repeat this process two more times. Top with a final layer of sauce.

Bake for 30 minutes. Increase the oven temperature to 425°F (220°C) and bake for an additional 15 minutes, until bubbling. Let stand for 10 minutes before serving.

Leftovers are excellent either warm or cold and can be stored, covered, in the fridge for up to 4 days.

# Delicious Fishes Dishes

**When it comes to dinner, I love fish in all of its fishy forms.**

I love tiny little silver anchovies swimming in briny oil next to some charred bread and a vermouth. I love fresh scallops, dug out of the sand at sunset and served raw with just a squeeze of lemon. I love big, meaty flatfish, slow roasted throughout the afternoon and eaten with hands for utensils, with fresh tortillas and bowls of vinegary summer tomatoes. I even love fried fish served out of a food truck on a bed of giant chips in a paper basket, washed down with white vinegar packets and cheap, cold beer.

Fish, for me, is a good-mood food. There's something about a fish dish that has a sense of adventure to it. It is so versatile. It has, as they say, range. You can do very little to it and serve it cold, as in Scallop Crudo in Herby Buttermilk (page 174), or you can do more to it but still not *that* much—this isn't that kind of cookbook—and cook up some Cod and Zucchini in Curry Coconut Broth (page 195). It can be very elegant like my Eggs and Lobster Baked in Cream (page 188), more rustic as in Roasted Cod with Sweet Pepper Piperade and Saffron Aioli (page 196), or even somewhere in between like my Herb Stuffed Rainbow Trout (page 200).

There are also so many different kinds of fish out there to explore. Not just big versus little or lake versus ocean. You can use frozen fish, fresh fish, cured fish, and tinned fish, and they will all be very good choices because fish—on any occasion—is delicious.

# Tuna Tartare with Miso Lime Mayo and Crispy Rice

**Serves 4 to 6**

### Rice

2 tablespoons (30 mL) neutral oil,
  such as canola or grapeseed
1½ cups (375 mL) cooked long grain rice
Pinch of salt

### Mayonnaise

2 teaspoons (10 mL) white miso

Zest and juice of 1 lime

¼ cup (60 mL) Aioli (page 295) or
  prepared mayonnaise

### Tartare

Ice cubes

1 pound (450 g) raw sushi-grade tuna

1 lime

2 radishes, thinly sliced

1-inch (2.5 cm) piece of cucumber,
  thinly sliced

Small handful of pea shoots

When I worked on Nantucket, every once in a while some guy in a pickup truck would pull up to the back door of the prep kitchen and ask us if we wanted a whole tuna. We emphatically did. When your fish is that fresh, you really don't need to do too much to it. Sliced raw with a bit of extra-virgin olive oil and salt and pepper is a very good way to eat it. That's not quite a recipe (it's more of an experience), so here is how we served it in the restaurant, cut up into cubes and smothered in a miso and lime mayo with crispy rice and pea shoots for crunch. Since this is a cold dish, I like to put the platter I serve this on in the freezer for at least 10 minutes to give it a good chill. It is a small detail, but a nice one.

Place a large platter in the freezer to chill.

**Make the Rice:** Line a plate with paper towels. In a medium non-stick skillet over high heat, warm the oil. Once it starts to shimmer, add the cooked rice. Use a rubber spatula to press the rice into a single layer in the skillet. Cook for about 2 minutes, then reduce the heat to medium-high and cook for another 3 minutes. Reduce the heat to low. Continue cooking for 10 to 12 minutes, until the rice is golden brown and very crisp. Use a perforated spatula to lift the rice onto the prepared plate. Sprinkle with the salt. Let cool completely.

**Make the Mayonnaise:** In a small bowl, whisk together the miso and lime zest and juice. Add the aioli and whisk until fully combined.

**Make the Tartare:** Place about 1 cup (250 mL) of ice and a splash of water in a medium metal bowl. Place a smaller metal bowl on top. Using your sharpest knife, cut the tuna into ¾-inch (2 cm) cubes and place it in the smaller metal bowl. Once all the tuna is cut, add the mayonnaise and stir to coat. Break up the rice into 3-inch (8 cm) chunks and add it to the tuna mixture. Stir to combine; it's okay if the rice breaks up a bit more. Spoon the tuna mixture onto the chilled platter. Juice the lime over the tuna. Top with the radishes, cucumber, and pea shoots. Serve immediately.

# Scallop Crudo in Herby Buttermilk

## Serves 2 to 4

### Herby Buttermilk
½ cup (125 mL) buttermilk
½ cup (125 mL) fresh flat-leaf parsley
½ cup (125 mL) fresh basil
¼ cup (60 mL) fresh dill
1 teaspoon (5 mL) granulated sugar
1 tablespoon (15 mL) extra-virgin olive oil
Salt

### Scallops
Ice cubes
1 pound (450 g) sea scallops
1 tablespoon (15 mL) extra-virgin olive oil
Juice of 1 lemon
Pinch of salt

### To serve
Extra-virgin olive oil, for drizzling
1 watermelon radish, thinly sliced
1 lime radish, thinly sliced
1 teaspoon (5 mL) flakey salt
1 teaspoon (5 mL) pink peppercorns, crushed

In the summer, there is a span of at least a few weeks when it is so hot that the thought of even going near the oven is anathema to me. Simply being in the kitchen seems unbearable, so I do my best to make only very fast, very cold dishes, and this is one of them. The word "crudo" is Italian, and it literally means "raw." Typically, a crudo is a combination of a fresh raw fish with some olive oil and citrus to add fat and flavour. Here, buttery raw scallops are thinly sliced and then drizzled with olive oil and lemon juice, but with the added bonus of a cooling, herby buttermilk-based broth. Buy the best scallops you can find and keep them as cold as possible before serving. As with Green Gazpacho with Salmon and Cucumber (page 125), Tuna Tartare with Miso Lime Mayo and Crispy Rice (page 173), and basically any cold dish, I recommend chilling the bowls you plan to serve it in to improve both the flavour and the experience of this simple, but significant dish.

Depending on how many people you plan to serve, place 2 to 4 small bowls in the freezer to chill.

**Make the Herby Buttermilk:** Place the buttermilk, parsley, basil, dill, and sugar in a high-speed blender and pulse to combine. With the blender running on low speed, slowly stream in the olive oil until fully combined. Add salt to taste. Pulse to combine. Store the buttermilk in the fridge until ready to serve.

**Make the Scallops:** Place about 1 cup (250 mL) of ice and a splash of water in a medium metal bowl. Place a smaller metal bowl on top. Using your sharpest knife, thinly slice the scallops and place them in the smaller metal bowl. Drizzle with the olive oil, lemon juice, and salt. Toss to combine.

**To serve:** Divide the buttermilk among the chilled bowls. Place the scallops on top and drizzle them with olive oil. Top each serving with radish slices and sprinkle with flakey salt and peppercorns. Serve immediately.

# Chili Shrimp and Butter Lettuce Salad

## Serves 4 to 6

### Shrimp

6 lime leaves (optional)

1 pound (450 g) large uncooked
    peel-on shrimp

Ice cubes

### Dressing

2 teaspoons (10 mL) fish sauce

Zest and juice of 2 limes

2 tablespoons (30 mL) Pickled Chilies
    (page 291), plus ¼ cup (60 mL) brine

2 tablespoons (30 mL) neutral oil,
    such as canola or grapeseed

### Salad

2 heads of butter lettuce

½ cucumber, chopped

½ daikon, sliced

2 avocados, pitted, peeled, and sliced

3 lime leaves, julienned

½ cup (125 mL) fresh mint

When I was in my twenties, I travelled to Thailand and basically ate my way across Bangkok. Fish sauce, lime leaves, and chilies were everywhere, and I really was in heaven because each of these ingredients, which make up a sort of Thai trinity, is loaded with flavour. A little goes a long way because when you combine them, they are more than the sum of their parts. Here, they are paired with barely poached shrimp, crispy butter lettuce, creamy avocado, crunchy vegetables, and of course some fresh herbs. The result is the kind of salad that doesn't need any sides but happens to still taste casually amazing next to Pan Seared Ribeyes with Ramp and Anchovy Butter (page 241) or even a simple, icy platter of Oysters and Hot Vinegar (page 21).

**Cook the Shrimp:** Bring a large saucepan of salted water to a boil. Remove the saucepan from the heat. Add the lime leaves (if using) and shrimp. Cover and let stand for 6 to 7 minutes, until the shrimp turn pink and are opaque. Meanwhile, prepare an ice bath by filling a medium bowl halfway with cold water and topping it with enough ice to make it shockingly cold. Drain the shrimp. Immediately plunge the shrimp into the ice bath and let stand for 10 minutes. Peel and devein the shrimp and transfer them to a clean plate. Place the shrimp in the fridge until you are ready to assemble the salad.

**Make the Dressing:** In a small bowl, whisk together the fish sauce, lime zest and juice, pickled chilies and brine, and oil.

**Assemble the Salad:** Gently tear the butter lettuce into large bite-size pieces. Place the lettuce in a large bowl or on a deep platter. Top with the cucumber, daikon, avocado, lime leaves, and about half of the mint and shrimp. Toss to combine. Add about three quarters of the dressing and toss again gently to coat. Top the salad with the remaining mint and shrimp and another drizzle of dressing. Serve immediately.

# Trout Salad with Yogurt and Jammy Eggs

**Serves 2 to 4**

### Salad

Large handful of green beans

4 eggs

1 medium head of Boston lettuce

2 cans (3.2 ounces/90 g each) trout in olive oil (I like Scout Canning)

½ cup (125 mL) fresh flat-leaf parsley, roughly chopped

¼ cup (60 mL) fresh dill, roughly chopped

Juice of 1 lemon

1 teaspoon (5 mL) Aleppo pepper

Salt, to taste

### Dressing

½ cup (125 mL) full-fat Greek yogurt

1 tablespoon (15 mL) extra-virgin olive oil

1 tablespoon (15 mL) water

Pinch of salt

This isn't a niçoise salad per se, but it is niçoise-like in that it calls for fish, green beans, and eggs—and you really would not be compromising its integrity if you added some thinly sliced, gently boiled potatoes or olives.

I like how simple this salad is, and how it comes together quickly just as I have needed it to on more than one occasion. Once you set your mind on it, all you have to do is put a saucepan of water on for the beans and eggs and then gather the rest of the ingredients. You'll have something fresh and filling in the time it takes an egg to get jammy.

**Start the Salad:** Bring a medium saucepan of salted water to a boil. While you're waiting for the water to boil, fill a medium bowl halfway with water and ice.

Drop the green beans into the boiling water and stir once to make sure they are all submerged. Blanch for 3 to 5 minutes, until the beans are bright green and crisp tender. Using tongs, immediately transfer the beans to the ice bath to chill. Once they are fully cooled, transfer them to a colander to drain.

Bring the water back to a boil and carefully lower in the eggs. Reduce the heat to medium so that the eggs are not rattling around too much in the water. Cook for 7 minutes at a gentle boil, then place the eggs in the ice bath. Let cool for 5 minutes. Peel the eggs.

**Make the Dressing:** In a small bowl, whisk together the yogurt, olive oil, water, and salt.

**Finish the Salad:** Lay the lettuce out on a large plate or in a shallow bowl. Spoon the trout and its oil on top. Cut the green beans and eggs in half and arrange them on top. Drizzle the dressing overtop and sprinkle with the parsley and dill. Drizzle with the lemon juice and season with the Aleppo and salt. Serve immediately.

# Potato Rösti with Labneh and Marinated Mackerel

## Serves 2 to 4

### Mackerel

2 cloves garlic, smashed

1 teaspoon (5 mL) Aleppo pepper

1 teaspoon (5 mL) granulated sugar

1 red Thai chili, halved

3 tablespoons (45 mL) white vinegar

¼ cup (60 mL) neutral oil, such as canola or grapeseed

2 cans (4 ounces/115 g each) boneless skinless mackerel packed in olive oil (I like Gold Seal)

### Rösti

1 pound (450 g) starchy potatoes, such as Idaho or russet

1 teaspoon (5 mL) salt

1 to 2 tablespoons (15 to 30 mL) neutral oil, such as canola or grapeseed

### To serve

½ cup (125 mL) labneh

Juice of 1 lemon

½ cup (125 mL) fresh dill, roughly chopped or torn

Cracked black pepper

A giant hash-brown type food slathered in yogurt and spicy marinated fish is the sort of thing I dream about. The crispy potato! The cold, creamy yogurt! The fiery mackerel! And then everything is served all together and covered in fresh lemon juice and dill! To me, it is a perfect dinner. I like to make the fish the day before so that it has time to really hang out in the spicy oil and absorb as much of the flavour as possible, but if you make it the day of, that's okay too. If you've never tried making a rösti, don't be intimidated. While it does take a little practice to get both sides evenly cooked and crispy, once you get the knack it's basically the equivalent of having a superpower because röstis are fast, inexpensive, and go great with a myriad of condiments and toppings.

**Marinate the Mackerel:** In a medium saucepan over high heat, whisk together the garlic, Aleppo, sugar, chili, and vinegar. Bring to a boil. Reduce the heat to low and simmer briefly, just until the sugar dissolves. Add the oil and whisk to combine. Remove the saucepan from the heat. Add the mackerel and its oil. Stir to combine. Let cool to room temperature. Store the fish and liquid in an airtight container in the fridge until ready to serve.

**Make the Rösti:** Line a large plate with paper towels. Heat a non-stick skillet over high heat. Working quickly so that the potatoes do not oxidize, peel the potatoes and use a box grater to grate them into a medium bowl. Sprinkle with the salt. Toss to combine.

Add about 1 tablespoon (15 mL) of the oil to the skillet. When it just starts to shimmer, add the potatoes. Using a perforated spatula, press the potatoes into a large, flat potato pancake. Cook, undisturbed, for about 1 minute, then reduce the heat to medium-high. Continue cooking for another 3 minutes. Reduce the heat again to medium and continue cooking for another 2 to 3 minutes until the potato is golden brown and crispy. Increase the heat to high and carefully flip the potato pancake. If this is

*recipe continues*

your first time flipping a rösti, you can give it your best shot with all the confidence you've got. Or, if you want to be careful and ensure that it doesn't fall apart, use the perforated spatula to carefully lift the rösti onto a dinner plate. Place an inverted dinner plate on top of the rösti to create sort of a rösti-plate sandwich and flip the rösti between the plates. If the skillet looks dry, add another 1 tablespoon (15 mL) of oil, then slide the now upside-down rösti back into the hot skillet. Cook the second side in the same manner as the first. Transfer the rösti to the prepared plate. Let cool for a few minutes.

**To serve:** Transfer the rösti to a large, rimmed plate. Spoon and spread the labneh onto the hot rösti. Place the mackerel on top. Drizzle some of its marinade on top. Squeeze the lemon juice over the fish. Garnish with the dill and lots of black pepper, to taste. Serve immediately.

Store leftovers in an airtight container in the fridge for up to 4 days.

# Mussels with Sausage, Pernod, and Toast

**Serves 4**

1 tablespoon (15 mL) unsalted butter or neutral oil, such as canola or grapeseed

4 ounces (115 g) sweet fennel sausage, casing removed

1 leek, thinly sliced

1 clove garlic, finely grated

Pinch of salt

¼ cup (60 mL) Pernod

2 pounds (900 g) mussels, cleaned

½ cup (125 mL) low-sodium chicken or vegetable stock

1 cup (250 mL) heavy (35%) cream

2 Roma or vine tomatoes, diced

2 tablespoons (30 mL) minced fresh chives

2 tablespoons (30 mL) chopped fresh tarragon

2 tablespoons (30 mL) chopped fresh chervil

2 tablespoons (30 mL) chopped fresh flat-leaf parsley

Charred bread, to serve

My first line cook job was at the Halifax Alehouse. The servers wore "medieval" bar wench costumes in various shades of clay, and a cover band played the same set list every Friday and Saturday, kicking off with "Folsom Prison Blues." The first thing I learned to make was dill mayonnaise, which was (and maybe still is?) the restaurant's signature sauce. The recipe was as simple as combining a medium bowl full of industrial mayonnaise with some lemon juice and enough dried dill to make it speckly but not green. The second thing I learned to make was these mussels, which are just slightly more complicated but, honestly, not much. Pernod and mussels are a classic pairing, and adding sweet fennel sausage to this combo really makes these mussels special. As always, I like to add a ton of herbs. Here, instead of bringing freshness, they add depth of flavour and harmony to the stock. Truly, I have never had a better mussel.

In a Dutch oven or large stockpot with a lid over high heat, melt the butter. Once it starts to bubble, add the sausage and cook for 2 to 3 minutes, stirring occasionally, until it browns. Add the leek and cook for 1 to 2 minutes, until softened. Add the garlic and salt. Stir to distribute.

If you're using a gas stove, move the Dutch oven away from the burner flame so that you don't accidentally flambé yourself. Carefully add the Pernod. Allow the alcohol to cook down for 30 seconds, then quickly add the mussels and stock. Cover and let the mussels steam for about 4 to 5 minutes, until they have opened. If they aren't opening, give them a stir. Sometimes if there are too many mussels in the pot, they may not have enough space to open.

*recipe continues*

Once the mussels are just opened, uncover and add the cream. Cook, uncovered, for 1 minute. Turn off the heat. Discard any mussels that have not opened; they are not edible. Add the tomatoes and about half of the herbs. Stir to combine.

Serve the mussels in the Dutch oven or transfer them to a large bowl. Top with the remaining herbs. Serve immediately alongside charred bread, a nice big bowl for empty shells, and a wad of paper napkins.

Should you have leftover mussels, I recommend removing them from their shells, discarding the shells, and returning the mussels to the broth before storing them in an airtight container in the fridge for up to 3 days.

# Puttanesca Helper

**Serves 4 to 6**

1 pound (450 g) cavatappi pasta

1 can (4 ounces/115 g) sardines packed in chili oil

2 cloves garlic, smashed

¼ cup (60 mL) capers

¼ cup (60 mL) black olives, pitted

1 can (8 ounces/225 g) whole tomatoes, roughly chopped

½ cup (125 mL) water

½ cup (125 mL) fresh flat-leaf parsley, roughly chopped

½ cup (125 mL) Bread Crumbs (page 289)

I've never eaten Hamburger Helper, but eight-year-old me always wanted to. The mascot, a happy little glove, was so friendly. There have been many times as a thirtysomething when I wished he would show up and make dinner just like in the commercials. I like to channel that spirit when I make this meal, which has nothing to do with "hamburger" but does rely on the same-shaped pasta. For a more grown-up flavour profile, this recipe uses a whole can of sardines packed in spicy oil, capers, and toasted bread crumbs. This dish is always a crowd-pleaser, but my daughters love it as well because cavatappi pasta, which is shaped like a corkscrew, is very fun to eat.

Bring a large saucepan of salted water to a boil. Cook the cavatappi according to package instructions, less 2 minutes. Drain. Spread the pasta out on a baking sheet so it cools but does not stick together.

Drain the spicy sardine oil into a large skillet and set the sardines aside. Heat the oil over medium-high heat. Add the garlic, capers, and olives. Cook for 1 minute. Add the tomatoes and their liquid. Cook for 1 to 2 minutes to get rid of the tomatoes' raw taste. Add the water and the pasta and cook for 2 minutes, stirring so that the pasta is evenly coated in the sauce. Turn off the heat but leave the skillet on the burner. Add the sardines and stir to break them up a bit. Let rest for 2 to 3 minutes, until the sardines warm through.

Sprinkle the parsley and bread crumbs overtop. Serve with your favourite throwback playlist.

Store leftovers in an airtight container in the fridge for up to 5 days.

# Eggs and Lobster Baked in Cream

**Serves 4 to 6**

1 can (3 ounces/90 g) Scout Canning lobster

1 clove garlic, smashed

3 cups (750 mL) baby spinach, roughly chopped

1 cup (250 mL) heavy (35%) cream

½ cup (125 mL) freshly grated Parmesan cheese, divided

Salt and cracked black pepper

4 to 6 eggs

2 tablespoons (30 mL) minced fresh chives

Charred bread, to serve

This is the sort of dish that feels luxurious even though you can pull the ingredients together and make it in about 15 minutes. With all that extra time, you can pour yourself a crisp glass of unoaked Chardonnay and linger over dinner with lots of crusty bread and a good companion or even just a good book. I suggest using Scout lobster because it's very high quality. It's harvested and hand-packed on Prince Edward Island, covered in butter, and canned. Even though it's a tinned product, it still tastes incredibly fresh and "of the sea," and in this recipe it eliminates the need to boil and clean a lobster on your own.

Preheat the oven to 400°F (200°C).

Place a medium ovenproof skillet with a lid over medium-high heat. Drizzle in the butter from the canned lobster. Add the garlic and sauté for 2 to 3 minutes, until fragrant. Add the spinach and cover for about 1 to 2 minutes, until the spinach has wilted. Add the cream and turn off the heat but leave the skillet on the burner so that the cream cooks down slightly. Sprinkle with about half of the Parmesan. Add salt and pepper to taste. Stir to combine.

Using a spoon, make small, evenly spaced wells in the cream and spinach mixture. Crack an egg into each well. Transfer the skillet to the oven. Bake for 8 to 10 minutes, until the whites of the eggs are set and the yolks are still creamy.

Top with the lobster, the remaining cheese and chives. Serve hot alongside charred bread.

# Clams and Kielbasa

**Serves 4**

2 tablespoons (30 mL) neutral oil, such as canola or grapeseed

8 ounces (225 g) kielbasa sausage, sliced

2 cups (500 mL) green cabbage, chopped

2 cloves garlic, finely grated

4 pounds (1.8 kg) fresh clams (Manila or littleneck), cleaned and rinsed

2 cups (500 mL) low-sodium chicken stock

½ cup (125 mL) full-fat sour cream

Salt and cracked black pepper

¼ cup (60 mL) fresh dill, roughly chopped

½ cup (125 mL) fresh flat-leaf parsley, roughly chopped

Juice of 1 lemon

Charred rye bread, to serve

My daughters love kielbasa, and I always keep it around because it's easy to make them off-brand Lunchables on the fly when I don't have anything else to feed them. I started using it more just because it was there but discovered that it's a great substitute for other sausages, and even bacon, in many recipes. It's smoky and porky but also a little sweet—and it tastes amazing braised, fried, or grilled. Clams and bacon are a classic pairing, so this is a little play on that, but with more of the Eastern European flavours I love.

In a Dutch oven or large stockpot with a lid over high heat, heat the oil. Add the kielbasa and cook for 2 to 3 minutes, stirring occasionally to prevent scorching, until lightly browned. Add the cabbage and cook for an additional 2 to 3 minutes, until softened. Add the garlic and stir to combine. Quickly add the clams and stock. Cover and let the clams steam for 4 to 5 minutes, until they have opened. If they aren't opening, give them a stir. Sometimes if there are too many clams in the pot, they may not have enough space to open.

Once the clams are just opened, remove the pot from the heat and add the sour cream. Stir to combine. Discard any clams that have not opened. They are not edible. Add salt and pepper to taste. Top with the dill and parsley, a few extra grinds of pepper, and a squeeze of lemon juice. Serve immediately alongside charred rye bread.

Leftover clams can be removed from their shells and refrigerated in an airtight container for up to 3 days.

# Corn, Bacon, and Mussel Chowder

**Serves 4 to 6**

4 ounces (115 g) thick-cut bacon

1 small white onion, thinly sliced

1 tablespoon (15 mL) unsalted butter

2 tablespoons (30 mL) all-purpose flour

½ cup (125 mL) dry white wine

8 ounces (225 g) new potatoes, sliced about ¾ inch (2 cm) thick

4 cups (1 L) seafood stock, warm

12 ounces (340 g) frozen, cooked, shelled mussels, thawed

2 ears corn, kernels removed and cobs discarded

1 cup (250 mL) cherry tomatoes, halved

1 cup (250 mL) heavy (35%) cream

2 cups (500 mL) arugula

Salt and cracked black pepper

As someone who has spent much of her life a few steps from the ocean, I had to include a seafood chowder in this book. I don't make chowder often, but when I do, a wave of homesickness crashes over me and I feel compelled to dim the lights, put on an old fisherman's sweater, and play a Stan Rogers album. For me, chowder is a mood. As far as the actual chowder goes, I like mine a bit lighter than your typical winter seafood chowder. The cherry tomatoes add little pops of freshness, the corn brings some brightness, and any time I can wilt greens into something, I do. The arugula adds both a freshness and a peppery note and breaks up the richness of the cream, potatoes, and seafood.

Line a plate with paper towels. In a large Dutch oven over high heat, cook the bacon. Once it starts to brown, reduce the heat to medium and continue cooking for 2 to 3 minutes, until it starts to render. Reduce the heat to low, cover, and continue cooking for 2 to 3 minutes, until the bacon is crisp. Using a slotted spoon, transfer the bacon to the prepared plate.

Add the onion and butter to the bacon fat remaining in the Dutch oven. Increase the heat to medium-high. Cook the onion for 3 to 4 minutes, stirring occasionally so it does not brown, until softened. Sprinkle the flour onto the onions. Stir to get rid of any lumps. Let cook for 2 to 3 minutes until the bacon fat has absorbed the flour.

Stirring continuously, add the wine. Cook for 3 to 4 minutes, until the liquid reduces by about half. Add the potatoes and the warm stock. Cover and bring to a boil. Reduce the heat to low and simmer for about 8 to 10 minutes, until the potatoes are tender. Add the mussels, corn, tomatoes, and cream. Stir to combine. Once everything is warmed through, turn off the heat and add the arugula. Cover for 1 minute to let the arugula wilt. Season with salt and pepper to taste. Serve immediately.

Store leftovers in an airtight container in the fridge for up to 3 days.

# Cod and Zucchini in Curry Coconut Broth

**Serves 4 to 6**

2 cans (14 ounces/400 mL each) full-fat coconut milk, plus ½ can water

2 tablespoons (30 mL) neutral oil, such as grapeseed or canola

2-inch (5 cm) piece of ginger, sliced

3 cloves garlic, smashed

1 tablespoon (15 mL) Jamaican yellow curry powder

1 teaspoon (5 mL) ground turmeric

1 green bird's eye chili, halved

5 lime leaves

2 tablespoons (30 mL) granulated sugar

2 tablespoons (30 mL) fish sauce

1 green or yellow zucchini, quartered lengthwise, then cut into 2-inch (5 cm) lengths

½ pound (225 g) cod, cut into 2-inch (5 cm) cubes

2 Roma tomatoes, chopped

**To serve**
Cooked jasmine rice or rice noodles
Fresh green chilies, thinly sliced
Handful of fresh basil, chopped
Handful of fresh cilantro leaves, chopped
Roasted peanuts, chopped
Lime wedges

I used to make this for staff meal on Nantucket using leftover fish trimmings. Because Nantucket is more or less a seasonal destination, the staff was from all over the world, and many of us were on student and work visas. There were a lot of different palates and preferences among the Irish, Canadians, Jamaicans, Nepalese, and Lithuanians. Of all the dishes I made, everyone loved this one the most. Even now, many years later, I think of it as being a dish that is full of good energy and happiness.

Open the coconut milk and place the cans near the stove.

In a large saucepan or Dutch oven over high heat, heat the oil until it just shimmers. Add the ginger and garlic and cook for 1 to 2 minutes, stirring continuously so they do not burn. Reduce the heat to medium. Add the curry powder and turmeric. Toast the spices for 1 to 2 minutes, stirring continuously so they do not burn. Add the coconut milk plus ½ can water, chili, lime leaves, and sugar. Increase the heat to high. Bring to a boil, then reduce the heat to low. Let simmer for 5 minutes.

Remove the saucepan from the heat but leave the burner on. Fish out and discard the ginger, garlic, and lime leaves. Add the fish sauce. Return the stock to the heat. Add the zucchini and let simmer for 3 to 4 minutes, until it's softened but still has a slight crunch. Gently add the cod and simmer for 1 minute. Turn off the heat and add the tomatoes. Let stand for 1 to 2 minutes, until the tomatoes warm through.

Ladle the curry over rice or noodles. Top each serving with chilies, basil, cilantro, peanuts, and lime wedges for squeezing.

Store leftovers in an airtight container in the fridge for up to 4 days.

# Roasted Cod with Sweet Pepper Piperade and Saffron Aioli

### Serves 4 to 6

**Piperade**

2 tablespoons (30 mL) extra-virgin olive oil

1 yellow onion, thinly sliced

2 red bell peppers, sliced

2 yellow bell peppers, sliced

2 tablespoons (30 mL) white vinegar

¼ cup (60 mL) water

Pinch of granulated sugar (optional)

2 cloves Garlic Confit (page 286), mashed with a fork, plus a drizzle of its oil

**Saffron Aioli**

1 clove Garlic Confit (page 286), plus a drizzle of its oil

½ cup (125 mL) Aioli (page 295)

Pinch of saffron, bloomed in 2 tablespoons (30 mL) hot water

**Cod**

1 (1½ to 2 pounds/675 to 900 g) cod fillet

1 teaspoon (5 mL) salt

2 tablespoons (30 mL) 00 flour (optional)

2 tablespoons (30 mL) neutral oil, such as canola or grapeseed

Lemon wedges, to serve

I make this dish of stewed peppers, a saffron-spiked aioli, and seared cod in the summer or fall when peppers are at their sweetest (and cheapest). Cod can be difficult to sear because it sticks to the skillet. To ensure that the cod fillet stays intact, I give it a quick dusting of 00 flour. If you'd rather not, just make sure your pan is ripping hot and that you pat your fish dry.

**Make the Piperade:** In a large skillet with a lid over high heat, warm the olive oil. When it starts to shimmer, add the onion and reduce the heat to medium. Cook for 3 to 4 minutes, stirring occasionally, until softened. Add the peppers and cover. Continue cooking for 5 to 7 minutes, stirring occasionally, until the peppers have softened. Add the vinegar, water, sugar (if using), and garlic confit and its oil. Cook for another 2 to 3 minutes, until the water has reduced and the peppers are soft. Transfer the piperade to a large platter.

**Make the Saffron Aioli:** Place the garlic confit and its oil in a small bowl. Mash it with a fork. Add the aioli and saffron water. Stir to combine. Place the bowl on the platter or spoon the sauce directly onto one end of the platter.

**Cook the Cod:** Cut the fish into 3- to 4-inch (8 to 10 cm) pieces. Thoroughly pat the fish dry with paper towels. Season with the salt. Sprinkle the flour (if using) on a large dinner plate. Roll each piece of fish in the flour.

Wipe out the large skillet you used to make the piperade. Return the skillet to high heat and add the oil. When the oil starts to shimmer, carefully place the fish in the skillet. Let the fish cook undisturbed for about 5 minutes, until it starts to caramelize. If the oil starts to smoke, reduce the heat to medium-high. Carefully flip each piece over, tilting the pan away from you so as not to splash any oil. Continue cooking the fish for another 3 to 5 minutes, until it is just cooked through. Transfer the cooked cod to the platter with the piperade and aioli. Garnish with lemon wedges for squeezing over the fish. Serve immediately.

Store leftovers in an airtight container in the fridge for up to 3 days.

# On Fresh Herbs

I love fresh herbs. For me, a handful of small herbs or even larger ones that have been roughly torn add so much appeal to a dinner. They look pretty, of course, particularly when used in abundance and especially if you happen to throw in a few edible flowers like nasturtiums or pansies. They can also add a tremendous amount of flavour and even excitement to a dish, whether scattered on top or tucked inside a meal.

There is something unmistakably *of the garden* about fresh herbs. Even if you are serving salad out of a bag or reheating a cast iron skillet full of leftovers, a few sprigs of torn basil leaves have the potential to breathe new life and a sense of freshness into an otherwise drab meal. So, considering they're relatively inexpensive, and even cheaper if you grow your own, keeping a mix of fresh herbs on hand is a must for me.

If you are new to the world of herbs, I recommend experimenting with them. Start with something like Every Night Salad (page 53) or Fried Cheese Salad (page 117), where they are mixed with other greens. Notice how the flavours of the ingredients around the herbs change, and how much fresher and brighter the whole dish tastes. Depending on the herbs you use, you can soften a dish with a lot of acidity like Celery with Walnuts, Feta, and Dill (page 62), balance out spicy flavours as the parsley does in Lamb Meatballs over Garlicky Labneh (page 233), or even cut through richness by using a mixture of herbs as in Salt Cod Brandade with Herb Salad (page 25).

For peppery flavour and a bit of crunch, use lots of roughly chopped fresh flat-leaf parsley. Dill, which has a lovely, almost licorice-y sweetness to it, can be torn and tucked into salads. Mint has the potential to be strong, so a little goes a long way, but the leaves, either whole or torn in half, are wonderful in spicier and richer dishes, both cooked and raw. Basil, which is so balanced in its sweet and savoury flavour profile, is best friends with summer produce like tomatoes, peppers, peaches, and zucchini and is so mild it can be used liberally. There are many other fresh herbs out there, so this list is not exhaustive, but in general these are the ones I reach for most often. As you continue to cook with herbs, I hope you'll find yourself leaning on them more and more, not just as something to add a pop of colour or to garnish, but as an integral part of making a cohesive and craveable dish.

# Herb Stuffed Rainbow Trout

**Serves 4 to 6**

1½ to 2 pounds (675 to 900 g) scaled and gutted rainbow trout
Salt and cracked black pepper
Extra-virgin olive oil, for drizzling
1 lemon, sliced
Small handful of fresh flat-leaf parsley
Small handful of fresh dill

A whole stuffed trout is impressive, but it is such a straightforward dish to prepare. And yet you will dazzle—yes, dazzle!—your dinner guests when you set this simple, elegant, hot, flakey fish bursting with parsley and dill on the table. Serve it alongside a plain green salad or some Butter Beans in Salsa Verde (page 29), or even just put it out with Chili Crisp (page 288) or Tartar Sauce (page 295) and crusty bread.

Preheat the oven to 450°F (230°C). Line a rimmed baking sheet with parchment paper.

Place the fish on the prepared baking sheet. Season it all over and inside the cavity with salt and pepper. Drizzle the fish generously with olive oil. Stuff the cavity with the lemon slices and herbs.

Bake for 16 to 20 minutes, until the flesh flakes easily and it is just cooked through. Serve immediately, or a little later if you like. The trout will hold up at room temperature for an hour or so, and it will be impressive no matter what.

Store leftovers in an airtight container in the fridge for up to 2 days.

# Salmon in Parchment with Peas and Rosé

**Serves 4**

½ small yellow onion, thinly sliced

1 cup (250 mL) shelled fresh peas

1 cup (250 mL) shelled fava beans

2 green onions, thinly sliced

4 tablespoons (60 mL) unsalted butter

¼ cup (60 mL) dry rosé wine

4 (6-ounce/170 g) centre-cut salmon fillets

1 teaspoon (5 mL) salt

Lemon wedges, to serve

**Tip:** *If the parchment paper has been sealed correctly, it should puff up, but if it doesn't that's not critical. You want the fish to be just cooked through.*

In culinary school, cooking "en papillote" is something we had to practise again and again—the recipe we used for this technique of baking fish in a parchment parcel also involved cutting tiny, perfect juliennes of leeks, peppers, and carrots to lay on top of the fish just so. In my kitchen at home I like a less precious preparation that involves fewer knife cuts while remaining true to the feel of this dish. Although I wouldn't call my version effortless, it's definitely less fussy. This recipe pairs salmon with favas and peas, which is a classic combination, and using a little rosé wine as the cooking liquid makes this a beautiful spring dish. Because the fish is inside the packet, it's difficult to tell if it has cooked through, but you can either wing it and hope for the best as I do or carefully open one packet to check that the fish is to your liking. Salmon is fairly forgiving—if it's a little over- or undercooked, no one will complain.

Preheat the oven to 400°F (200°C).

Cut 4 rectangles of parchment paper, each approximately 16 × 12 inches (40 × 30 cm). Spread the rectangles out on a large work surface (they can overlap slightly), folding up the edges of the rectangles a bit since you'll be adding liquid to them.

Divide the yellow onion, peas, beans, green onion, butter, and wine evenly between the 4 rectangles, placing them in a little mound just left of centre. Place a salmon fillet on top of each mound. Season with the salt. Fold the bottom right corner of the rectangle over the fish to the top left corner of the rectangle to make a triangle. Roll up the open edges of each parchment triangle to seal them. Carefully transfer the packets to a large rimmed baking sheet. Bake for 8 to 10 minutes.

Carefully transfer the packets onto dinner plates. Serve immediately alongside a dish of lemon wedges. Let your guests tear into their packets at the table but be sure to let everyone know not to eat the paper!

Store leftovers in an airtight container in the fridge for up to 3 days.

# Tomato Roasted Salmon

**Serves 6 to 8**

1 jar (8 ounces/225 g) sundried tomatoes packed in oil

5 cloves Garlic Confit (page 286), plus a drizzle of its oil

1 tablespoon (15 mL) capers

1 tablespoon (15 mL) white vinegar

¼ cup (60 mL) fresh flat-leaf parsley, briefly chopped

Extra-virgin olive oil, for drizzling

1 (2- to 3-pound/0.9 to 1.35 kg) salmon fillet

1 teaspoon (5 mL) salt

When you put this dish out, everyone will think you had your party catered. In a good way. It *feels* like something you would pay $200 for, but it's not. And even though blitzing up some tomatoes and spreading them on a fish is fairly straightforward, it feels a bit special too.

Place the tomatoes, garlic confit and its oil, capers, and vinegar in a high-speed blender and pulse to combine. Unplug the blender and, using a rubber spatula, scrape down the sides of the jar to make sure everything is well mixed. Plug in the blender again. Add the parsley and pulse again a few times. Set aside.

Preheat the oven to 250°F (120°C). Line a rimmed baking sheet with parchment paper and drizzle it with olive oil.

Lay the salmon on the prepared baking sheet, skin side down. Sprinkle with the salt. Drizzle it with a little more olive oil. Set the oven to broil. Broil for 15 minutes.

Remove the salmon from the oven and smoosh the tapenade over the flesh side of the fish. It doesn't have to be too neat, so don't be fussy. Reduce the oven heat to 250°F (120°C). Bake for another 10 to 15 minutes, until the fish is just cooked through. This dish is very good served hot, but it's also fine served at ambient temperature or even chilled.

Store leftovers in an airtight container in the fridge for up to 4 days. Leftovers are very good smashed onto crusty bread with thinly sliced cucumber and just a whisper of Aioli (page 295).

# Meat the Mains

**In my house, we don't eat meat with every meal or even every day.**

This has nothing to do with how I feel about meat, which is generally very favourable, but I find purchasing quality meat to be expensive. This makes sense when you consider the care and cost associated with raising an entire animal, and I would rather eat it a little less often and buy the best quality I can afford. To put it bluntly, you can buy an awful lot of cabbages for the price of a grass-fed steak.

There are times, however, when it seems nothing but a charred meaty entrée for dinner will do. On those evenings, I go all in and make something like Flank Steak with Salsa Verde and Cumin Smashed Potatoes (page 239) or Pan Seared Ribeyes with Ramp and Anchovy Butter (page 241).

I tend to gravitate toward serving dishes family-style when I have these cravings. When it comes to eating, I find that a few slices or half of a chop is more than enough for me, especially when the large-format meats I often cook are presented alongside a thoughtful salad and some vinegar-soaked vegetables.

There are also times when the comfort of a good meaty braise or a stew are required. I cannot deny the necessity of having a recipe like Harissa Chicken (page 213) or Crispy Chicken Thighs over Vinegar Beans (page 214) in my back pocket. Or, if you crave meat as I do, with a lighter touch that leaves me feeling satiated but not over-the-top full and maybe nestled alongside the contrasting crunch of something green and verdant, then go ahead and make Steak Salad with Pepperoncini and Green Goddess Dressing (page 235) or Lamb Meatballs over Garlicky Labneh (page 233). Whatever your meaty mood, there is something dinner-worthy in this section for you.

# Spring Chicken Soup

**Serves 4 to 6**

1 Hot Honey Roast Chicken (page 210)
   or store-bought rotisserie chicken

2 tablespoons (30 mL) extra-virgin
   olive oil, more for drizzling

1 medium yellow onion, chopped

3 stalks celery, chopped

1 bunch green Swiss chard, leaves
   and stems separated and chopped

2 bunches red radishes, halved

2 teaspoons (10 mL) salt, more to taste

8 cups (2 L) chicken stock

1 handful each of fresh dill, tarragon,
   and parsley

I was in no way obligated to include a chicken soup recipe in this book, but there are recipes I feel compelled to share because they will improve your life. Am I being hyperbolic? Probably, yes, but if there was ever something to hyperbolize over, I think it's chicken soup. Chicken soup is a Very Important Soup because it makes great use of all the leftovers from a roast chicken, and it makes you and your people feel cared for in a way that is both rare and necessary in today's world. Chicken soup is brothy and thoughtful and something to linger over, together or alone, with a napkin in your lap and a smile on your lips. This soup has all the hallmarks of a great chicken soup and takes only a small effort to put together. If you want to make the effort smaller still, feel free to use a pre-roasted rotisserie chicken from the grocery store.

Remove all the meat from the chicken and chop it into bite-size pieces. Set aside.

In a large stockpot or Dutch oven over medium-high heat, warm the olive oil. Add the onion, celery, chard stems, and radishes. Season with the salt. Cook for 3 to 4 minutes, stirring occasionally so that the vegetables do not brown, until everything has softened slightly.

Add the stock, cover, and bring to a boil. Reduce the heat to low and let simmer for 10 to 15 minutes, until the vegetables are tender but not mushy. Add the chicken and cook for 1 to 2 minutes, until it is warmed through. Turn off the heat. Stir in the chard leaves. Garnish with the dill, tarragon, and parsley. Season to taste with salt. Serve immediately with a drizzle of olive oil.

Store leftovers in an airtight container in the fridge for up to 4 days.

# Hot Honey Roast Chicken

**Makes 1 roast chicken**

1 small chicken (about 2 to 3 pounds/
0.9 to 1.35 kg), room temperature

Salt and cracked black pepper

2 tablespoons (30 mL) sweet paprika

½ small yellow onion

½ lemon

2 to 3 red long chilies

3 cloves garlic, smashed

½ cup (125 mL) Hot Honey (page 293),
more to serve

Well-seasoned, piping hot, and juicy, roast chicken regularly lands on my dinner table, and regardless of whether the occasion is casual everyday eating or a special event, for me it is always a highlight. This roast chicken recipe requires no great effort to get ready. Rubbing sweet paprika all over the skin before popping it in a 500°F (260°C) oven ensures that it will come out looking absolutely amazing, and the smell from the chilies, garlic, and onion stuffed in the cavity is beyond enticing. The whole chicken gets smothered in spicy-sweet hot honey to finish, and believe me when I say you will need to put out extra napkins—it's just that good.

Preheat the oven to 500°F (260°C). Spray a medium roasting pan with cooking spray (this will make cleanup easier). Weigh your chicken and make a note of how many pounds it is.

Liberally sprinkle the whole chicken with salt and pepper, inside and out. Sprinkle the paprika all over the chicken, using your hands to rub it into the skin. Stuff the cavity with the onion, lemon, chilies, and garlic. If there is an excess of skin or fat around the cavity, trim it off and discard.

Nestle the chicken into the pan. There is no need to truss or tie it. Roast for 10 minutes per pound, plus 5 to 10 minutes, or to an internal temperature of 165°F (74°C). If you don't have a thermometer, that's okay. I don't have one either. Just give a thigh a little poke with a paring knife and check to make sure the juices run clear.

Brush liberally with the hot honey. Let the chicken rest at room temperature for 10 to 15 minutes. Using your favourite spoon, give the chicken a final baste with any pan juices before serving. Serve warm, with extra hot honey for drizzling and dipping.

Store leftovers in an airtight container in the fridge for up to 5 days.

# Harissa Chicken

## Serves 4 to 6

### Sauce

4 red bell peppers, cored and roughly chopped

2 cloves garlic, smashed

1 red or green long chili, seeded

1 cup (250 mL) low-sodium chicken stock or water

### Chicken

4 bone-in chicken legs, separated

Salt and cracked black pepper

1 tablespoon (15 mL) sweet paprika

2 tablespoons (30 mL) extra-virgin olive oil or ghee

¼ cup (60 mL) Harissa (page 296), to serve

This dish is on heavy rotation in my house because it requires minimal prep and only a few ingredients. Plus, it's so delicious and goes with just about anything. I like to spoon it over jasmine rice, but it's also great served with some fluffy flatbread or crispy potatoes. The sauce is mild enough for my daughters, and for anyone who is spice-averse the chili can be left out. Or you can serve it with a big bowl of plain yogurt and some extra lemon wedges to help balance the heat.

**Make the Sauce:** Place the peppers, garlic, chili, and a splash of stock in a high-speed blender. Pulse to combine. With the blender running on high speed, stream in the remaining stock until fully incorporated and smooth.

**Cook the Chicken:** Preheat the oven to 350°F (180°C). Pat the chicken dry and season all over with salt, pepper, and the paprika.

Place the olive oil in a deep skillet or Dutch oven over medium-high heat. Arrange the chicken, skin side down, in the skillet. Sear for 4 to 5 minutes, until the skin is crispy and golden. Flip and cook on the other side for 3 minutes. Transfer the chicken to a clean plate. Pour all but about 2 tablespoons (30 mL) of the rendered chicken fat and oil into a small bowl and reserve for future use (see page 10 for suggestions). Add the sauce to the skillet. Reduce the heat to medium and let cook for 2 to 3 minutes so that the sauce thickens and any raw taste is cooked out.

Return the chicken, skin side up, to the skillet and transfer it to the oven. Bake, uncovered, for 20 to 25 minutes until the chicken is cooked through or reaches an internal temperature of 165°F (74°C). Remove the chicken from the oven and drizzle the harissa overtop. Serve immediately.

Store leftovers in an airtight container in the fridge for up to 4 days.

# Crispy Chicken Thighs over Vinegar Beans

**Serves 4 to 6**

6 bone-in chicken thighs or 3 legs, separated

Salt and cracked black pepper

1 tablespoon (15 mL) neutral oil, such as canola or grapeseed

1 medium yellow onion, thinly sliced

2 cloves garlic, finely grated

1 red bird's eye chili, split

½ cup (125 mL) dry white wine

2 tablespoons (30 mL) white wine vinegar

2 cans (14 ounces/400 mL each) butter beans, drained and rinsed

1 cup (250 mL) low-sodium chicken stock

½ cup (125 mL) large green olives

Pinch of granulated sugar (optional)

1 whole lemon

This dish feels very French to me, for no particular reason, I suppose, other than that it's brothy and rather beige. While those descriptors may not be for everyone, to me, brothy and beige is beautiful. I love this recipe for a quick and straightforward dinner. Chicken thighs are my favourite part of the chicken, and here they are well seasoned and fried until the skin renders and is juicy and crisp. The thighs are then set aside while onions, wine, butter beans, citrus, and olives are quickly introduced to each other in the same hot pan. Then the chicken is returned before everything gets placed in the oven so that the chicken cooks through while the other flavours deepen and catch all the chicken juices. Simple, but so good. *Mais oui!*

Preheat the oven to 350°F (180°C).

Pat the chicken dry and season all over with salt and pepper. In a deep ovenproof skillet or Dutch oven over medium-high heat, heat the oil. Add the chicken, skin side down. Sear until the skin is crispy and golden, about 4 to 5 minutes. Flip and cook on the other side for 3 minutes. Transfer the chicken to a clean plate. Pour all but about 2 tablespoons (30 mL) of the rendered chicken fat and oil into a small bowl and reserve it for future use (see page 10 for suggestions).

Reduce the heat to medium, add the onion to the skillet, and cook for 2 to 3 minutes, stirring to prevent browning. Add the garlic and chili and cook for 1 minute. Increase the heat to high. Add the white wine and let it reduce for 2 to 3 minutes. Add the vinegar, beans, stock, olives, and sugar (if using). Using a vegetable peeler, remove the peel of the lemon in large strips. Add the peel to the skillet.

Return the chicken, skin side up, to the skillet and transfer it to the oven. Bake, uncovered, for 20 to 25 minutes, until the chicken is cooked through or reaches an internal temperature of 165°F (74°C). Remove from the oven and squeeze the lemon overtop. Serve immediately.

Store leftovers in an airtight container in the fridge for up to 4 days.

# Butter Bean and Corn Chicken Stew

**Serves 6 to 8**

2 tablespoons (30 mL) extra-virgin olive oil

1 medium yellow onion, diced

1 medium red bell pepper, diced

1 medium orange bell pepper, diced

1 green long chili, sliced

1 tablespoon (15 mL) salt, more to taste

1 teaspoon (5 mL) ground cumin

1 teaspoon (5 mL) ground oregano

1 teaspoon (5 mL) ground coriander

6 cups (1.5 L) chicken stock

2 to 3 cups (500 to 750 mL) cooked chicken or store-bought rotisserie chicken, diced

2 cans (14 ounces/400 mL each) giant butter beans

2 ears of corn, kernels removed and cobs discarded

**To serve**

Lime wedges

Crystal hot sauce, or your preferred brand

Full-fat sour cream

This is one of my favourite recipes to make as summer winds down and cooler temperatures are upon us. Slightly thicker than a soup, thanks to the puréed vegetables and beans added at the end, this stew leans on summer produce staples bell peppers and corn for delicious sweetness and also gorgeous pops of colour. The butter beans and chunks of chicken make this stew really filling, although it's so good I have a hard time saying no to second helpings.

Place the olive oil in a Dutch oven over high heat. Once the oil begins to shimmer, add the onion, peppers, chili, salt, cumin, oregano, and coriander. Reduce the heat to medium. Cook for 5 minutes, until the vegetables soften. Add the stock. Bring to a boil, then reduce the heat to just under medium. Add the chicken. Let simmer, covered, for 15 to 20 minutes, or until the vegetables are tender. Add the beans and corn. Cook for another 2 to 3 minutes until they are warmed through.

Carefully scoop out about 2 cups (500 mL) of the bean mixture (you want mostly beans, not liquid) and place it in a high-speed blender. Purée until smooth. Return the purée to the stew and stir to combine. Season with salt to taste.

Divide the stew among bowls and serve with lime wedges, hot sauce, and sour cream.

Store leftovers in an airtight container in the fridge for up to 4 days.

# Everyone
# to the Table

The thing about dinner is that people of all ages have to eat it, including very young people, who, I will admit, are not always my target demographic when I'm planning to host a really amazing evening or even to just get a meal on the table. My daughters, now five years old, certainly have their preferences. While I'm happy they want to share their opinions and ideas about most things with me, there are moments when I wish these opinions and ideas—which can sometimes be categorized as *strong feelings*—would stop when it comes to the plates I put in front of them.

But I also get it. Watching my daughters make decisions and express themselves is a good thing, even if it's just about whether the Hot Honey Roast Chicken (page 210) is *too close* to the Caesar Beans (page 57) or about the Creamy Radish Dip (page 34), which they've declared "not dippy enough." To me, this all seems like not a big deal. In their lives, though, it *is* a big deal, and I try to remember that. For me, creating a dinner that everyone will enjoy might take a few extra moments of planning, but at the end of the day the payoff is sitting down with my children for a meal that is more or less peaceful.

Offering children the chance to choose what they eat might seem counterintuitive, and so I wouldn't necessarily suggest that. However, I think that curating an arsenal of kid-friendly recipes goes a long way toward maintaining equilibrium at the dinner table. You can begin normalizing different types of foods and flavours, even if they aren't immediately met with enthusiasm. When I'm looking to introduce something new, I try cooking a dish that includes something familiar, such as cheese or noodles. Hominy is not a food I grew up eating, but if my mother had set a hot, bubbling platter of Hominy Cab 'n' Cheese (page 98) on the table, I guarantee you I would have. Ditto for Pumpkin Stuffed Shells with Brown Butter Béchamel (page 165), and really, what child could possibly resist Toad in the Hole (page 223), which features golden brown sausages sunk in a giant, puffy, golden Yorkshire Pudding–adjacent batter.

I am also, I will admit, not above a "rebrand" when it comes to convincing my children to get on my level—it's not Lemony Spaghetti Squash with Burrata and Herbs (page 68), it's, uh, pasta with white cheese. No, no, no, that's not Charred Eggplant Dip (page 33), that's hummus. You love hummus! Finally, in a nod to further autonomy, when I'm looking to entice my daughters to really dig into dinner, it does help if there's some sort of action or assembly required. I truly believe this is why Lunchables are so popular. Snack boards, similar to one you might make for yourself, are always met with excitement, but so are things that have a dipping element, such as Paprika Sweet Potatoes with Lime Crema (page 93) or even (!) Salt Cod Brandade with Herb Salad (think about it: it's essentially an inside-out fish stick once you put it on toast) (page 25).

I don't like to tell people exactly how to feed their kids, because I do think it's a really personal choice, but what I will say is that children are not children forever, and I do want to soak up as much of the joy of this time as possible. If that means eating Garlic Fingers (page 46) slightly more often than I normally would to placate their palates and avoid fits of tears, well, so be it. Do what seems reasonable for them, but also for you. They won't remember exactly what you served, but they will remember the way you made them feel.

# Toad in the Hole

**Serves 4**

1 teaspoon (5 mL) extra-virgin olive oil

5 large pork sausages

1¼ cups (300 mL) whole milk (3.25%)

1 cup (250 mL) all-purpose flour

4 eggs, beaten

1 tablespoon (15 mL) Dijon mustard

Large pinch of kosher salt

½ cup (125 mL) shredded Gruyère cheese

My family moved to England in 1987. If you love carbs and sausages, it was a glorious time to live in the UK. So much of the culinary landscape at that time was beige and brown, and I was in my own personal gastronomical heaven. I still remember the first time I encountered Toad in the Hole during school lunch. It was amazing to me that someone would think to take something that was already so perfect and delicious like a sausage and then embed it in hot, tender, yolky, crispy Yorkshire pudding and make it *even better*. To this day I think TITH is a culinary triumph. It may feel even more like one in North America because people will think you're making them some sort of egg fried in toast. When you set this dish on the table, everyone will be amazed and clap for you. You will feel like a star. Or, at the very least, they will love it and you will feel a bit smug, which is just as good.

Preheat the oven to 475°F (240°C).

In a large cast iron skillet or Dutch oven over high heat, warm the olive oil. Once it starts to shimmer, add the sausages and cook for 2 to 3 minutes on each side, reducing the temperature to medium if they start to get too dark, until they are golden brown all over. Remove the sausages from the skillet and place the skillet in the oven to heat up for 5 minutes.

Meanwhile, in a medium bowl, whisk together the milk, flour, eggs, Dijon, and salt until well combined. Add the cheese. Whisk to combine.

When the skillet is smoking hot, quickly open the oven door, return the sausages to the skillet, and pour all the batter overtop. Bake for 30 to 35 minutes, until golden brown and puffy and the centre is still a bit custardy. Serve immediately.

# Mapo Tofu with Greens

**Serves 4 to 6**

1 pound (450 g) medium ground pork

1-inch (2.5 cm) piece of ginger, minced

2 cloves garlic, minced

1 teaspoon (5 mL) salt

Pinch of ground red chilies

1 tablespoon (15 mL) neutral oil,
such as canola or grapeseed

1 tablespoon (15 mL) low-sodium
soy sauce or tamari

2 cups (500 mL) low-sodium chicken
or vegetable stock

1 tablespoon (15 mL) cornstarch

1 tablespoon (15 mL) oyster sauce

1 teaspoon (5 mL) sesame oil

½ teaspoon (2 mL) granulated sugar
(optional)

1 bunch kale, washed and torn into
bite-size pieces

½ cup (125 mL) Chili Crisp (page 288),
more to serve

1 pound (450 g) soft or medium-firm
tofu, drained and cubed

Cooked long grain rice

2 scallions, thinly sliced

I make this as a comfort food dish when I want something substantial and a bit spicy. I love how the thick sauce clings to the pork, and the way the soft, creamy tofu offers a break from both the spice and the texture of the other ingredients. Adding loads of kale at the end is not traditional, but it's how I make it in my house, so I've included it here as well. You can swap out the kale for an equal amount of spinach or bok choy if you like; those greens are also delicious.

In a medium bowl, using your hands or a wooden spoon, combine the pork, ginger, garlic, salt, and chilies.

In a large skillet or wok over high heat, heat the oil until it just shimmers. Add the pork mixture, pressing it down with the back of a spoon so that it becomes a large, flat pork pancake. Reduce the heat to just over medium. Cook for 2 minutes, until the pork develops a deep brown crust. Carefully flip over the pork pancake. Sear the second side in the same way.

Add the soy sauce and break up the meat with your spoon. In a medium bowl, whisk together the stock and cornstarch. Add it to the pork, along with the oyster sauce, sesame oil, and sugar (if using). Cook for 5 minutes, stirring occasionally, until the sauce has thickened. Turn off the heat. Stir in the kale, chili crisp, and tofu. Cover and let stand for a few minutes, until the kale has wilted and the tofu has warmed through.

Serve over long grain rice. Garnish with scallions and more chili crisp on the side.

Store leftovers in an airtight container in the fridge for up to 4 days.

# Maple Pork Chops over Apple Fennel Slaw

**Serves 2 as a main
or 6 as a side**

### Pork Chops

2 cups (500 mL) hot water

¼ cup (60 mL) kosher salt

¼ cup (60 mL) granulated sugar

½ cup (125 mL) ice

2 (1½ inch/4 cm thick) bone-in
   pork chops

1 tablespoon (15 mL) neutral oil,
   such as canola or grapeseed

1 tablespoon (15 mL) unsalted butter

2 tablespoons (30 mL) pure maple syrup

Small handful of fresh thyme sprigs
   (optional)

### Slaw

1 tablespoon (15 mL) white vinegar

2 tablespoons (30 mL) Aioli (page 295)
   or prepared mayonnaise

Pinch of sugar

Pinch of celery seed

2 Granny Smith apples, thinly sliced

1 bulb of fennel, thinly sliced

I love a pork chop. Meaty, tender, juicy, and with just a little bit of chew—they are so good. Brining pork chops helps season them from the inside out and keeps them moist. Here, I finish them with just *a little* butter and some maple syrup. You can serve these whole, but I prefer to slice them and serve them over this creamy slaw. They are also delicious with Braised Red Cabbage with Cider and Bacon (page 85) and Celery with Walnuts, Feta, and Dill (page 62)—and maybe a hunk of bread.

**Make the Pork Chops:** In a non-reactive container, whisk the hot water with the salt and sugar until they dissolve. Add the ice and stir to melt.

Place the pork in the brine. Refrigerate for at least 1 hour, up to 4 hours. Remove the pork from the brine. Using paper towels, pat it dry. Set aside at room temperature to take the chill off.

In a large heavy-bottomed skillet over high heat, add the oil. Once it starts to shimmer, lay the chops gently in the pan. Cook the chops for 2 to 3 minutes on each side, until a dark brown crust develops. If the oil starts to smoke, reduce the heat slightly so that the chops do not burn. Reduce the heat to medium and transfer the chops to a plate. Tip the oil out of the skillet. Return the chops to the skillet. Add the butter, maple syrup, and thyme (if using). Using your favourite big spoon, baste the chops. Continue basting over medium heat for another 2 to 3 minutes until the pork is just cooked through. Transfer the chops to a cutting board and let rest while you make the slaw.

**Make the Slaw:** In a medium bowl, whisk together the vinegar, aioli, sugar, and celery seed. Add the apples and fennel. Toss to combine.

**To serve:** Transfer the slaw to a large plate or divvy it up among individual plates. Slice the pork chops about ½ inch (1 cm) thick and place them on top of the slaw along with any juices from the cutting board. Serve immediately.

Store leftovers in an airtight container in the fridge for up to 4 days.

# Crispy Pork over Many Coloured Tomatoes and Stracciatella

**Serves 4**

### Pork

1 pound (450 g) pork loin, cut into 1 inch (2.5 cm) thick cutlets

½ cup (125 mL) all-purpose flour

2 eggs, beaten

1 tablespoon (15 mL) Dijon mustard

1 tablespoon (15 mL) water

1 cup (250 mL) panko bread crumbs

1 tablespoon (15 mL) salt, divided, more to finish

1 cup (250 mL) neutral oil, such as canola or grapeseed

### Tomato Salad

2 pounds (900 g) mixed tomatoes, quartered, with their juice

2 heads of baby gem lettuce, leaves separated

8 ounces (225 g) stracciatella cheese

Extra-virgin olive oil, for drizzling

Salt and cracked black pepper

Hot Honey (page 293), for drizzling

I like foods that taste like other foods. In this case, there is just a *hint* of a BLT vibe happening. Crispy pork bites, juicy tomatoes and lettuce, and a little creamy something from the stracciatella mingle to create a harmonious dish. Each ingredient is enhanced by the ones around it. Breading the cutlets does take a minute or two, but the reward is worth it. Since there are so few ingredients in this dish, I suggest you buy (or grow) the best tomatoes you can find. It's worth it to invest. When you are cutting them, collect the juice and spoon it over the salad for a boost of tomato flavour.

**Make the Pork:** Lay the pork cutlets on a clean cutting board. With a firm grip on a rolling pin, give each cutlet a few whacks so that it is roughly ¾ inch (2 cm) thick. Get 3 medium bowls; place the flour in the first; the eggs, Dijon, and water in the second; and the bread crumbs in the third. Divide the salt among the 3 bowls. Stir each mixture with a fork to ensure that it's combined.

Working quickly, dip each cutlet in the flour, give it a shake, dip it in the egg wash, give it a shake, and then dip it in the bread crumbs. Using your hands, make sure each cutlet is fully coated and press the bread crumbs into the egg wash. Place the breaded cutlets on a clean plate.

Line a plate with paper towels. In a heavy-bottomed skillet over medium-high heat, heat the oil until it just shimmers. Working one or two at a time, fry the cutlets for 2 to 3 minutes on each side, until crispy and golden. Transfer the cutlets to the prepared plate, sprinkle with salt, and let rest. Repeat until all the cutlets have been cooked.

**Make the Tomato Salad:** On a large platter, lay out the tomatoes and lettuce. Tear the cheese into bite-size pieces and scatter overtop. Spoon any tomato juice overtop and drizzle generously with olive oil. Season all over with salt and pepper to taste. Slice the pork into 1-inch (2.5 cm) pieces and transfer it to the platter. Drizzle everything with hot honey and serve immediately.

# Lamb Loin Chops over Minty Pistachio Butter

**Serves 4 to 6**

Lamb loin chops look like mini T-bone steaks, and they are the perfect size for me, especially when nestled alongside some Prosciutto Wrapped Eggplant (page 142), Fried Cheese Salad (page 117), or even Zucchini and Feta Flatbread with Harissa and Pine Nuts (page 49). The pistachio butter used in this recipe is not exactly a sauce, but more of a creamy, nutty landing pad for the lamb. It is so good you will want to make extra and schmear it on flatbread, plunk roasted fish in it, or dollop it onto charred vegetables.

### Pistachio Butter

1 cup (250 mL) pistachios
2 tablespoons (30 mL) pistachio oil
1 tablespoon (15 mL) white miso
Zest and juice of 2 limes
Handful of fresh mint
½ cup (125 mL) ice water

### Lamb

8 to 9 bone-in lamb loin chops
Salt and cracked black pepper
1 tablespoon (15 mL) neutral oil, such as grapeseed or canola
1 tablespoon (15 mL) white vinegar

### To serve

Juice of 1 lime
½ cup (125 mL) fresh mint, chopped or torn
2 tablespoons (30 mL) pistachios, toasted and chopped (see Toasted Nuts, page 290)
Pink peppercorns, crushed

**Make the Pistachio Butter:** Place the pistachios, oil, miso, lime zest and juice, and mint in a high-speed blender. Pulse to combine. With the blender running on high speed, slowly add the ice water. Purée until smooth. Store the pistachio butter in an airtight container in the fridge until ready to use.

**Cook the Lamb:** Line a plate with paper towels. Season the lamb all over with salt and pepper.

In a large skillet over high heat, heat the oil until it just shimmers. Working in batches, sear the chops for 1 to 2 minutes on each side until they develop a dark brown crust. Transfer to the prepared plate.

Once all the chops have been seared, turn off the heat. Tip out the oil and discard. Return the chops to the skillet. Add the vinegar and toss the chops to coat.

**To serve:** Dollop the pistachio butter in the centre of a large plate. Using a spoon, push the pistachio butter from the centre of the plate to the edges, making a nice landing pad for the lamb. Arrange the lamb on the pistachio butter and squeeze the lime juice overtop. Garnish with the mint, pistachios, and crushed peppercorns. Serve immediately.

Store leftovers in an airtight container in the fridge for up to 4 days.

# Lamb Meatballs over Garlicky Labneh

**Serves 4 to 6**

### Pita Chips

1 pita bread, torn into 2-inch (5 cm) pieces

1 tablespoon (15 mL) extra-virgin olive oil

1 teaspoon (5 mL) Aleppo pepper

1 teaspoon (5 mL) sumac

Pinch of salt

### Labneh

4 cloves Garlic Confit (page 286), plus a drizzle of its oil

1 cup (250 mL) labneh

### Meatballs

1 pita bread, torn into 2-inch (5 cm) pieces

¼ cup (60 mL) whole milk (3.25%)

2 cloves Garlic Confit (page 286), mashed with a fork

1 pound (450 g) ground lamb

1 teaspoon (5 mL) salt

1 teaspoon (5 mL) Aleppo pepper

1 teaspoon (5 mL) cumin

1 teaspoon (5 mL) coriander

1 tablespoon (15 mL) neutral oil, such as canola or grapeseed

If a meatball dish could ever be described as "fresh," it's this one. Plonked in a puddle of garlicky labneh, covered in crunchy onions and pita, and then topped with loads of parsley and lemon, this lamb meatball dish is bursting with bright flavours. Make these on a summery evening and serve them alongside warm Turkish bread and a tin of stuffed grape leaves or put them out as part of a small feast with Spicy Oven Charred Cabbage and Lemons (page 152), Minty Smashed Chickpea and Plum Freekeh Salad (page 108), and Roasted Carrots with Tahini and Herbs (page 97).

**Make the Pita Chips:** Preheat the oven to 425°F (220°C). Line a rimmed baking sheet with parchment paper.

In a small bowl, toss the pita with the olive oil, Aleppo, sumac, and salt to coat evenly.

Spread the pita out on the prepared baking sheet. Bake for 5 to 6 minutes, until crispy and brown. Set aside. Increase the oven temperature to 475°F (240°C).

**Make the Labneh:** In a small bowl, use a fork to mash the garlic confit and its oil together. Add the labneh. Stir to combine. Set aside.

**Make the Meatballs:** Place the pita in a medium bowl. Add the milk and stir once. Let stand for about 10 minutes, giving it a poke a few times so that the pita soaks up the milk. Add the garlic confit and smash everything together with a fork until combined. Add the lamb, salt, Aleppo, cumin, and coriander. Using your hands, mix everything until just combined. Working quickly, divide the meatball mixture into 6 equal portions. Using your hands, form each portion into a ball.

*recipe continues*

**To assemble**

½ yellow onion

Pinch of salt

Pinch of sugar

1 teaspoon (5 mL) white vinegar

½ cup (125 mL) fresh flat-leaf parsley, chopped

1 teaspoon (5 mL) sumac

2 tablespoons (30 mL) toasted pine nuts (see Toasted Nuts, page 290)

Drizzle of extra-virgin olive oil

Juice of 1 lemon

Harissa (page 296), for drizzling (optional)

In a Dutch oven or large ovenproof skillet, heat the oil over high heat until it just shimmers. Place the meatballs in the hot oil. Sear all over, doing your best to keep them round-ish by turning them often. Transfer to the oven and bake for 15 minutes, or until the meatballs are just cooked through. They will still look slightly pink in the centre when they're done. If you prefer your meatballs to be well-done, leave them in for about 5 to 7 minutes longer, until they are grey all the way through.

**Assemble the dish:** Place the onion in a small bowl of ice water for about 10 minutes to remove the sting. Drain and return the onion to the bowl. Add the salt, sugar, and vinegar and massage briefly so that the seasonings are absorbed by the onion. Add the parsley, sumac, pine nuts, olive oil, and lemon juice. Toss to combine.

Using a large spoon, dollop the labneh onto a large plate or platter and schmear it into a large circle. Arrange the meatballs on top of the labneh. Top with the onion and herb mixture and the pita chips. Drizzle with the harissa (if using). Serve this dish hot or let it mellow a bit and serve it warm. Both ways are delicious.

Store leftovers in an airtight container in the fridge for up to 4 days. These meatballs are excellent sliced and stuffed into a pocketed bread with a handful of mint and a spoonful of Charred Eggplant Dip (page 33).

# Steak Salad with Pepperoncini and Green Goddess Dressing

**Serves 2 to 4**

### Dressing (makes 1 cup/250 mL)

1 cup (250 mL) loosely packed fresh basil

½ cup (125 mL) loosely packed fresh dill

½ cup (125 mL) loosely packed fresh flat-leaf parsley

1 tablespoon (15 mL) Dijon mustard

Juice of 1 lemon

¼ cup (60 mL) Aioli (page 295) or prepared mayonnaise

½ cup (125 mL) full-fat sour cream or plain yogurt

Cracked black pepper

### Salad

1 pound (450 g) skirt or strip steak (about 2 steaks)

2 tablespoons (30 mL) neutral oil, such as canola or grapeseed, divided

Salt and cracked black pepper

½ small white onion, thinly sliced

½ head of iceberg lettuce, chopped

1 cup (250 mL) pepperoncini, sliced, plus 1 tablespoon (15 mL) brine

1 tablespoon (15 mL) white vinegar

8 ounces (225 g) feta cheese, drained and crumbled

Large handful of fresh flat-leaf parsley, chopped

This is a great recipe to throw together effortlessly. Everything can be made in advance, and it takes only a few moments to combine. The recipe for the creamy, herb-packed dressing makes about 1 cup (250 mL), which is slightly more than you will need, but it can be kept in the fridge for up to 1 week. It has a myriad of uses (a dip! a spread! a dressing for something else!) and is a fan favourite despite how simple it is to make. The steak also can be cooked a day or two ahead, perhaps when your grill (or stovetop) is already on to cook something else. Just be sure not to slice it until you are ready to make the salad.

**Make the Dressing:** Place the basil, dill, parsley, Dijon, and lemon juice in a high-speed blender. Pulse to combine. Add the aioli and sour cream. Blend until smooth. Check the seasoning and add pepper, to taste. Pulse to combine. Transfer the dressing to an airtight jar and refrigerate until ready to use. Leftover dressing can be stored in this way for up to 1 week.

**Make the Salad:** Pat the steaks dry and place them in a shallow dish. Brush them all over with 1 tablespoon (15 mL) of the oil and season generously with salt and pepper (about a ½ teaspoon/2 mL salt per side and 3 to 4 grinds of pepper). Let rest at room temperature for about 30 minutes to improve how the meat sears. If the steaks are ice cold, they will cool down the pan and it will be difficult to develop a good, dark crust on the meat.

In a large heavy-bottomed skillet over high heat, heat the remaining 1 tablespoon (15 mL) oil. Once it starts to shimmer, gently lay the steaks in the skillet. If you have a splatter guard, you can cover the steaks while they cook to reduce mess. Cook for 2 to 3 minutes on each side, reducing the heat to medium if the oil starts to smoke, until a dark brown crust has developed and the steaks are cooked to just under medium, about 135°F to 145°F (57°C to 63°C). Transfer the steaks to a cutting board and let rest while you prepare the other ingredients.

*recipe continues*

Place the onion in a small bowl of ice water for about 10 minutes to remove the sting. Drain.

Meanwhile, place the lettuce, pepperoncini and brine, vinegar, and feta in a large bowl.

Slice the steaks into ½-inch (1 cm) wide pieces, against the grain. Add the onions, steak, and parsley to the salad. Toss to combine. Add about half of the dressing and check the seasoning. Add more dressing and black pepper to taste. Serve immediately.

# Flank Steak with Salsa Verde and Cumin Smashed Potatoes

**Serves 4 to 6**

Meat and potatoes! I mean, can you name a more iconic duo? I don't think so, and surely not one that has stood the test of time quite like M&P. Having an excellent recipe at your fingertips for this staple pairing is a must, and this one has enough low-effort, high-impact touches like an extremely herby and vinegar-laced salsa verde and super-crispy cumin potatoes to land it a permanent place on your dinnertime roster.

### Potatoes
1 pound (450 g) new potatoes
1 teaspoon (5 mL) baking soda
Salt
Extra-virgin olive oil, for drizzling
1 tablespoon (15 mL) cumin seeds

### Steak
1 to 1½ pounds (450 to 675 g) flank steak
2 to 3 tablespoons (30 to 45 mL) neutral oil, such as grapeseed or canola, plus more for frying
Salt and cracked black pepper
2 tablespoons (30 mL) unsalted butter
2 tablespoons (30 mL) red wine vinegar

### Salsa Verde
1 shallot, minced
2 tablespoons (30 mL) red wine vinegar
1 teaspoon (5 mL) granulated sugar
3 to 4 cloves Garlic Confit (page 286)
1 green chili
½ cup (125 mL) fresh cilantro
½ cup (125 mL) fresh flat-leaf parsley
¾ cup (175 mL) extra-virgin olive oil
Salt and cracked black pepper, to taste
Pinch of ground red chilies

**Make the Potatoes:** Preheat the oven to 475°F (240°C). Line a rimmed baking sheet with parchment paper.

Place the potatoes in a medium saucepan and cover with cold water. Sprinkle in the baking soda and some salt. Bring the potatoes to a boil over high heat. Reduce the heat to just above a simmer and cook for 7 to 10 minutes, until the potatoes are easily pierced with a paring knife. Drain. Set the potatoes aside until they are cool enough to handle.

Place the cooled potatoes on the prepared baking sheet. Using a dough knife or a small skillet, spatula, or clean kitchen towel, press down on the potatoes until the skin splits and they are about ¾ inch (2 cm) thick. Drizzle the potatoes with olive oil. Sprinkle them with a pinch of salt and the cumin seeds. Roast for about 10 to 15 minutes, until golden brown and crispy.

**Cook the Steak:** Pat the steak dry and place it in a shallow dish. Brush it all over with enough of the oil to coat and season generously with salt and pepper (about 1 teaspoon/5 mL salt per side and 3 to 4 grinds of pepper). Let rest at room temperature for about 30 minutes to improve how the meat sears. If the steak is ice cold, it will cool down the pan and be difficult to develop a good, dark crust on the meat.

*recipe continues*

In a heavy-bottomed skillet that is large enough to fit the steak, heat 1 tablespoon (15 mL) oil over high heat. Once it starts to shimmer, gently lay the steak in the skillet. If you have a splatter guard, you can cover the steak while it cooks to reduce mess. Cook for 2 to 3 minutes on each side, reducing the heat to medium if the oil starts to smoke, until a dark brown crust has developed. Reduce the heat to low and transfer the steak to a plate. Tip the oil out of the skillet and discard. Return the steak to the skillet. Add the butter and vinegar. Using your favourite big spoon, baste for another 2 to 3 minutes, until the steak is fully coated and only a little buttery vinegar remains in the pan. Transfer the steak to a cutting board and let rest while you prepare the rest of the dish.

**Make the Salsa Verde:** In a small bowl, whisk together the shallot, vinegar, and sugar, until the sugar dissolves. Add the garlic confit and use a fork to mash it into the shallot mixture. Add the green chili, cilantro, and parsley. Pour the olive oil overtop. Stir to combine. Season with salt, pepper, and the chilies. Give it a final stir to combine.

**To serve:** Transfer the potatoes to a large platter. Slice the steak into about ½-inch (1 cm) wide pieces, against the grain. Place it on top of the potatoes along with any juices. Spoon about one third of the salsa verde over the steak. Put the rest out in a bowl or jar so people can spoon more on if they like. Serve immediately.

Store leftovers in an airtight container in the fridge for up to 3 days.

# Pan Seared Ribeyes with Ramp and Anchovy Butter

## Serves 2 to 4

### Butter

¼ pound (115 g) ramps or scallions

¼ pound (115 g) unsalted butter, softened, divided

Pinch of salt

4 white anchovies, roughly chopped, plus a splash of brine

### Ribeyes

2 (12 ounces/340 g each) ribeyes

2 tablespoons (30 mL) neutral oil, such as canola or grapeseed, divided

Salt and cracked black pepper

2 tablespoons (30 mL) white vinegar

When I go for something like a steak, I want to fully commit to the experience. Minimal fuss and a little salt, pepper, acid, and some funky butter is all I need because, really, the focus should be on the meat.

During the early spring months, ramps—also known as wild leeks—grow in the woods near my house. They are so delicious sautéed or steamed with a drizzle of olive oil—or, as here, wilted and then mixed into a compound butter. You can take a quick peek online to see if they grow near you. Just be sure not to tug out the root when you harvest them so that they continue to grow for everyone. If you don't have access to ramps, or you're not confident foraging, scallions are a great substitute. This recipe yields more butter than you will need, but it freezes well. Use it to make amazing garlic bread or toss it on some warm New potatoes with a handful of fresh herbs.

**Make the Butter:** If you are using ramps, start by making sure they are really clean. Fill a sink with cold water and plunge the ramps in. Let them sit in the water for 5 to 10 minutes. Using your hands, agitate them to remove any grit and dirt. Shake off any excess water and dry them using a clean kitchen towel or paper towels. Trim off any root ends you may have accidentally tugged out (you can replant them!) and then separate the white stalk from the green leaf with a sharp knife. Chop the white part into ½-inch (1 cm) rounds. Cut the green parts into roughly 3-inch (8 cm) lengths.

In a medium skillet over medium-high heat, melt about 1 tablespoon (15 mL) of the butter. Once it begins to bubble, add the white parts of the ramps. Cook, stirring continuously so that they do not take on any colour, for about 1 minute. Add the green parts of the ramps and cook for an additional 1 minute, until they wilt. Season with the salt and let cool to room temperature.

Place the anchovies and brine in a medium bowl. Add the butter and ramp mixture. Using a rubber spatula,

*recipe continues*

mix the butter so that the ramps and anchovies are evenly distributed.

Lay a rectangle of parchment paper (about 12 × 8 inches/ 30 × 20 cm) on a clean work surface. Using the same spatula, dollop the butter into the centre. Roll the parchment around the butter to make a log about 2 inches (5 cm) in diameter. Place in the fridge until ready to use.

**Cook the Ribeyes:** Pat the steaks dry and place them in a shallow dish. Brush them all over with 1 tablespoon (15 mL) of the oil and season generously with salt and pepper (about ½ teaspoon/2 mL salt per side and 3 to 4 grinds of pepper). Let rest at room temperature for about 30 minutes to improve how the meat sears. If the steaks are ice cold, they will cool down the pan and it will be difficult to develop a good, dark crust on the meat. Slice the butter into ½-inch (1 cm) rounds.

In a large heavy-bottomed skillet over high heat, heat the remaining 1 tablespoon (15 mL) oil. Once it starts to shimmer, gently lay the steaks in the skillet. If you have a splatter guard, you can cover the steaks while they cook to reduce mess. Cook for 2 to 3 minutes on each side, reducing the heat to medium if the oil starts to smoke, until a dark brown crust has developed. Reduce the heat to low and transfer the steaks to a plate. Tip the oil out of the skillet and discard. Return the steaks to the skillet. Place a slice of butter (or two!) on each steak and baste using your favourite big spoon. Increase the heat to medium, add the vinegar to the skillet, and continue basting for another 2 to 3 minutes. Transfer the steaks to a cutting board and let rest while you make an Every Night Salad (page 53) or prepare some Oysters and Hot Vinegar (page 21).

Slice the steak into about ½-inch (1 cm) wide pieces, against the grain. Serve with more butter.

Store leftover steak in an airtight container in the fridge for up to 4 days. The butter can be kept in an airtight container in the fridge for up to 1 week or in the freezer for up to 3 months.

# Dinners I Remember

Sometimes it's the food that makes a dinner special. Other times it's the people, or the setting, or even the silence. A transcendent meal is never a specific dish, but rather an experience. Below I share a few of those special times, for no purpose other than to make sure that they are written down and to remind you that good times at the table are essential to a happy life.

**Grandma and the BLT**

I cannot tell you the exact department store that Grandma and I were in. If I had to guess, I'd say it was a Woodward's, but it's possible that we were in Hudson's Bay or Eaton's. It was the early 1990s, and we were on Vancouver Island in a store full of smartly dressed mannequins with a tidy but full housewares department and a sports equipment section that smelled like AstroTurf and hockey tape. We rode the escalator all the way to the top floor, making our way up, up, and smoothly arriving in a space that revealed itself to be a restaurant.

It had not occurred to me that such a thing was possible. A restaurant—where you sit down and use real cutlery and are served by a server. It felt terrifically luxurious and also convenient. Shopping does tend to be a hungry-making activity with all the walking and recycled air and coveting of expensive things.

My grandma, a creature of habit, told me she would order the BLT. I had never heard of a BLT. I had to ask her what it was. "Bacon, lettuce, and tomato," she explained. After some further explanation, and a promise of the inclusion of bread, I was curious enough to order the same thing. I'd had all the components before, just not together.

Eating them together was something I could not have imagined. The toasty white bread covered in more mayonnaise than I would have been permitted at home (my grandmother called it "dressing"), a crisp leaf or two of iceberg lettuce, juicy drippy tomatoes, and just enough salty, fatty bacon to make the entire sandwich a revelation. It was all just delicious.

**Liver in Nantes, France**

I sat on a little red futon in an apartment in Nantes. The small, icy glass of Pernod in my hand washed away any sense of fullness I felt from the cheese and sweets I had eaten when we went to the market.

As pieces of liver were gently lifted from the pan and set on a plate lined with a folded paper towel, I watched. I did not cook the liver, but I saw that it had been gently patted dry and then seasoned and seared until it was crispy on the outside and meltingly tender on the inside. Some crisp bits remained in the pan. A splash of Beaujolais was added to loosen them, and then butter was lovingly and efficiently whisked into the reduced wine by a handsome Frenchman to make a simple but ambrosial sauce. We each had a serving of liver doused in the butter sauce and ate it alongside some grape tomatoes that had been in the pan for no longer than was necessary—just enough to concentrate their flavour and take the chill off. It was a perfect meal, and we ate it in silence with the rest of the Beaujolais.

### Couldn't-Have-Been-Better Per Se

I was twenty-three and had never spent so much money on a meal. I made somewhere around minimum wage at the time, but I was frugal and had saved all my cash tips.

When we arrived, the server told us that Chef Thomas Keller was pleased that young cooks were coming to dine at Per Se, and that my friend Ali and I would be his VIP guests for the evening. We desperately tried not to giggle in front of him. We failed.

What I remember about that meal was the sense of luxury and even of excess. White truffles flying everywhere, the Sauternes served with rabbit and carrots becoming the most perfect nectar, the brioche (only half eaten) being whisked away because "it is only good when it is warm" and replaced with a fresh, buttery slice.

I still have the menu, as well as the feeling of having been treated so well by someone whose work I respect so much.

### A Meeting, a Meal

Nantucket in the spring is magical. It is quiet and foggy and wet. Thirty miles out to sea, with streets paved with cobblestones and lamplight that glows more yellow than it does on the mainland, it is otherworldly in the cool months of May and June. The history of the island, which is famous for its whaling ships and Quaker sentiments, is in everything. It's in the cedar shake houses, the battered leather furniture, and the smell of damp mould that catches you when you open a cupboard for the first time in a few days.

My friend Denis started the Nantucket Wine Festival from nothing: a few tables at the Siasconset Casino and some pals to help him pour wine. He had grown the festival to include some of the most incredible wineries in France and California. Somehow, I landed myself on the board of directors. We had a lot of meetings in the spring months, but few decisions were made. The festival simply chugged along, everyone tending to their own fires and putting them out when they inevitably flared. Meetings typically involved many people talking at once, and eventually Denis would get frustrated and abandon us for the kitchen to make a festive lunch.

On one particular day, when the air was damper than usual and the clouds threatened to release their rain, Denis left us to our spreadsheets and chatter earlier than usual and shuffled into the kitchen, where he was nurturing a massive pot of soup. Far from a stew, it was brothy and deeply golden, with minimal vegetables (Denis cannot tolerate anything green) and hunks of good sausage bobbing amicably alongside slivers of onions and garlic. Exhausted from all the chatter, I wandered into the kitchen to find Denis at the old enamel stove. A layer of steam fogged his glasses as he turned off the heat, and then his big chapped hands, somehow becoming tender, dropped whole cubes of foie gras into the pot. A final stir, then. The best wine was opened. The meeting was over. It was time to eat.

**Mutter Teller**

The winter I lived in Kreuzberg, Germany, I was very hungry. I had not made much of an effort to find a job. I had enough money to survive, but not always to eat. Unemployed and not a little bored, I walked a lot and eventually discovered a nearby outdoor market, which managed to be both familiar and strange at the same time. German winters are cold, and there was surprisingly little daylight. At times it could feel bleak, but a trip to the market, where I stole warmth from the crowding bodies jostling their heavy bags of apples, nuts, and pumpkins, softened the edges of the season.

I made it a habit to walk through the market the same way each time, and I knew all the regular vendors who jockeyed alongside each other with fresh produce, cheeses, meats, and a very good selection of Turkish-by-way-of-Germany foods like gözlemes, döners, and fried dough rings drenched in sugar syrup. Sometimes I would shell out whatever coins I had for a few crisp pears or a hard wedge of cheese, which I would take home and eat slowly, slice by slice, while I sat swaddled in sweaters in my chilly room.

One day, at the end of my second loop around the market, I saw a large Black woman wrapped in bright yellow wax print ladling food out of large pans into black plastic bowls. She was strikingly attractive, but it was the food she was serving that drew me to her. Everything looked so good, so different from everything else at the market, and I dug around in my pockets for my coin purse so I could have a taste.

When I ordered the Mutter Teller, I was deftly served, and the bowl was soon hot in my hands. I looked down at black-eyed peas swimming in tomato gravy. There were occasional smudges of dark leafy greens and a good amount of deep ruby–coloured oil. It was rich and warming on every level. Salty and crisp fried plantains shattered between my teeth before giving way to a creamy sweetness that was both intense and mellow at the same time. And then there were a few hunks of meat—maybe goat, maybe lamb. I could not tell, but it did not matter because they were so tender I ate them with a plastic spoon. To look at the food, it did not appear complicated, but everything that I could have wanted was there, and it was, and is, one of the most compelling dishes I have ever eaten.

# Just Desserts

**In my grandparents' house, there was always dessert after dinner.**

This may seem a bit indulgent at first blush. At my grandparents' house, the dessert was not necessarily fancy—a scoop of Chapman's ice cream on top of glistening cubes of ripe cantaloupe, or maybe a small square of deeply chocolate Toasted Walnut and Cacao Brownies (page 252)—but it was a sweet ending to complete the meal.

For most of my adulthood, I didn't give too much thought to dessert. I was often busy, and sitting down for meals was rare. My mind was typically not on the food in front of me but travelling forward in time to the next project, chore, or worry. But that's changed as I've given in to the rhythms of being a mother and accepted the need to be a force of calm for two little people who, since I met them, have been architects of chaos in my life.

What's "normal" has changed over the years, but many of the things I took for granted or that felt habitual have also shifted in ways that are both surprising and dramatic. There have been moments in the past few years when leaving the house has been impossible, when life seemed very bleak, and even when I felt so incredibly alone but somehow also couldn't bear to spend time with anyone or anything except perhaps a quiet and consoling slice of Marble Cake (page 269). And so, I have been eating more dessert than ever, and I'd like to encourage you to do the same. Sit down to eat, enjoy your meal, and say yes to a wedge of Apple Tart with Rose Cream (page 267).

My grandparents lived through difficult times. Yes, there was the Great Depression, and the Second World War, but also more personal and specific difficult times—barn fires, broken hearts, disease, death. From this I have taken strength, of course, but also recipes. Now, more than ever, I follow their example and enjoy the sweet things in life whenever I can.

# Dark Chocolate and Molasses Cookies

**Makes 12 large cookies**

½ cup (125 mL) unsalted butter, room temperature

¾ cup (175 mL) granulated sugar

2 tablespoons (30 mL) fancy molasses

1 large egg

2 teaspoons (10 mL) pure vanilla extract

½ teaspoon (2 mL) espresso powder

1¼ cups + 1 tablespoon (315 mL) all-purpose flour

2 teaspoons (10 mL) cornstarch

1 teaspoon (5 mL) baking powder

1 teaspoon (5 mL) baking soda

½ teaspoon (2 mL) kosher salt

1 cup (250 mL) dark chocolate chunks

I made a version of these by accident when I was trying to bake cookies with my daughters on a lazy Sunday. We were all out of brown sugar, so I added some molasses along with the white sugar. I was a bit heavy handed, and I worried that the cookies would taste too much like a molasses cookie. Instead, they turned out to be the most perfect, chewy, dare I say, *satisfying* chocolate chunk cookie I've ever made.

In a stand mixer fitted with the paddle attachment, cream the butter, sugar, and molasses on high speed until fluffy. Add the egg and vanilla. Add the espresso powder. Mix until well combined.

In a medium bowl, sift the flour, cornstarch, baking powder, baking soda, and salt. Add the dry ingredients to the butter and sugar mixture. On low speed, mix until just combined. Add the chocolate chunks. Stir to combine. Cover the dough and chill in the fridge for at least 2 hours, or overnight.

Preheat the oven to 350°F (180°C). Line a baking sheet with parchment paper. Remove the dough from the fridge and let it sit at room temperature for 10 minutes.

Roll the chilled dough into 1½- to 2-inch (4 to 5 cm) balls. Arrange them on the prepared baking sheet. Press each dough ball slightly to flatten. Bake for 8 to 10 minutes. Remove from the oven and slam the baking sheet once, sharply, against a hard (non-chippable) surface to help the cookies settle. Let cool on the baking sheet for 5 minutes. Transfer the cookies to a wire rack to cool completely.

Store the cookies in an airtight container at room temperature for up to 5 days.

# Toasted Walnut and Cacao Brownies

**Makes about sixteen 1½-inch (4 cm) square brownies**

1 cup (250 mL) walnut halves

¼ cup (60 mL) cacao nibs

½ cup (125 mL) unsalted butter, cubed

½ cup (125 mL) semi-sweet or dark chocolate chips

1 cup (250 mL) granulated sugar

2 large eggs

½ teaspoon (2 mL) pure vanilla extract

½ teaspoon (2 mL) kosher salt

¾ cup (175 mL) all-purpose flour

1 tablespoon (30 mL) black cocoa powder

These brownies are one of the first things from my grandma's recipe book that I learned how to bake. Over the years I've made a few tweaks, but there wasn't much to improve on. I like to use good-quality, organic walnuts here, and since I'm investing in the nuts, I want to coax as much flavour out of them as I can by toasting them. I also toast the cacao nibs, which brings out their fruitiness, makes them just a little crispy, and results in a brownie that is super dense and fudgy but studded with all kinds of wonderful textural surprises.

Preheat the oven to 325°F (160°C). Generously grease an 8-inch (2 L) square pan.

On a large baking sheet, spread out the walnuts and cacao nibs. Bake for 8 to 10 minutes, until fragrant.

In a medium saucepan over medium-high heat, melt the butter. Add the chocolate chips and remove the saucepan from the heat. Let stand for 1 to 2 minutes. Stir in the chocolate until smooth-ish but don't worry if a few chips don't melt all the way. Add the sugar, eggs, vanilla, salt, flour and cocoa stirring well to combine after each addition. Fold in the walnuts and cacao nibs.

Use a rubber spatula to transfer the mixture to the prepared pan. Bake for 20 minutes. These brownies will be very gooey. If you are looking for more of a cakey texture, bake for an additional 5 minutes. Let the brownies cool completely before serving.

Store leftovers in an airtight container in the fridge for up to 1 week.

# Caramel Pecan Ice Cream Crumble Cake

**Serves 10 to 12**

### Caramel

1½ cups (375 mL) granulated sugar

2 tablespoons (30 mL) water

½ cup (125 mL) unsalted butter, cubed

¾ cup (175 mL) heavy (35%) cream
 or crème fraîche

Pinch of salt

### Crumble

1 cup (250 mL) pecans, toasted and
 chopped (see Toasted Nuts, page 290)

1¾ cups (425 mL) all-purpose flour

1 cup (250 mL) brown sugar

1 cup (250 mL) rolled oats

½ pound (225 g) unsalted butter, melted

8 cups (2 L) good-quality vanilla ice
 cream, softened

There's a subset of desserts that could be categorized as "suitable for a potluck," and whenever I see one I make a beeline for it. Maybe it's the large format, maybe it's the homey ingredients—whatever it is, I love a Pyrex dish of sweet stuff. This dessert delivers all that and more. It has a cold creamy layer of vanilla ice cream sandwiched between a crunchy cookie crumble and a luscious topping of salty sweet caramel. You can make this in about as long as it takes to bake the crumble, and if you're in a rush, no one will know if you swap out the homemade caramel for a decent store-bought version and add a pinch of salt.

**Make the Caramel:** In a medium heavy-bottomed saucepan over medium-high heat, combine the sugar and water. As the sugar begins to melt, whisk so that it does not burn. Keep whisking until all the sugar is melted and then stop, allowing the sugar to caramelize. If one spot seems like it's getting particularly dark, you can swirl the saucepan, but in general you want to leave it alone so that it caramelizes evenly. When the melted sugar turns an amber colour, add the butter and whisk to combine. Remove the saucepan from the heat and let rest for 1 minute. Slowly pour the cream into the caramel and add the salt. Whisk to combine. Let cool.

Preheat the oven to 400°F (200°C). Line a rimmed baking sheet with parchment paper.

**Make the Crumble:** Place the pecans, flour, sugar, and oats in a large bowl. Add the melted butter and mix well. Press the mixture into the bottom of the prepared baking sheet. Bake for 7 minutes. Stir briefly. Bake for an additional 8 minutes, until golden brown. Let cool to room temperature.

**Assemble the Dessert:** Press half of the cookie crumble into a 13- × 9- inch (3.5 L) baking dish. Spread the ice cream overtop in an even layer. Top with the remaining cookie crumble. Pour the caramel evenly on top. Cover and store in the freezer until ready to serve.

Store tightly covered in the freezer for up to 2 weeks.

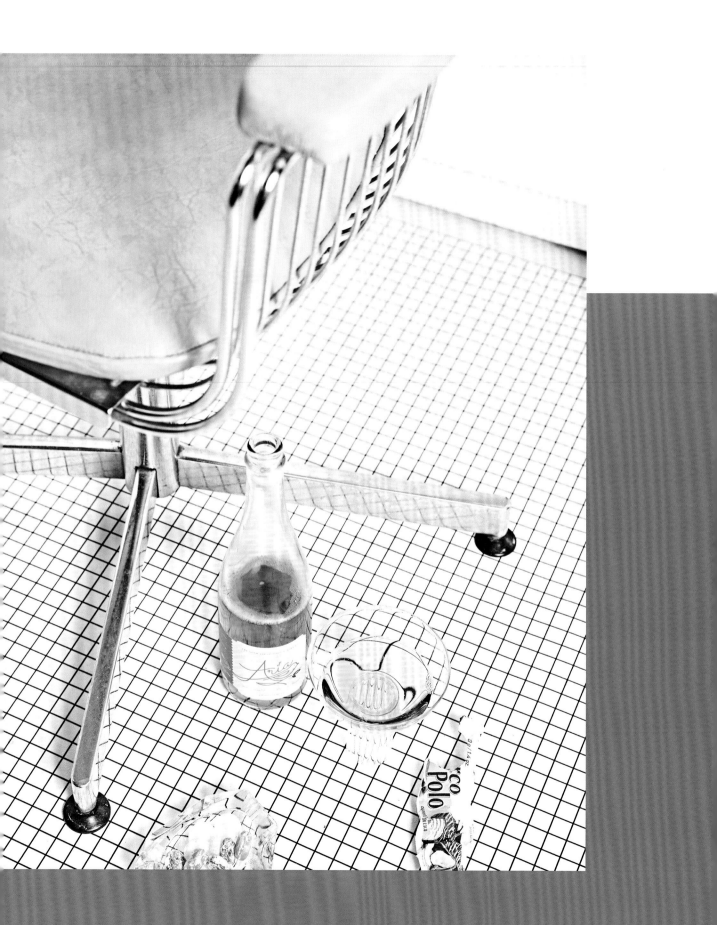

# The Joy
# of Eating Alone

When people ask me to describe this book, I always say that it's very much a personal cookbook because it's true to how I eat at home. I have a feeling, and I hope you agree, that many other people would like to eat as I do—often simply, but with big flavours and a lot of textures.

There are lots of cookbooks that celebrate eating together and being together and throwing big, wonderful parties, but I think there's something really special and really wonderfully indulgent about eating dinner alone, especially when you make exactly the thing you want to eat, the way you want to eat it, and then eat it however feels best to you. For me, someone who often talks all day long and cares for people, whether they are guests at my restaurants or my own children, there is a tremendous amount of satisfaction in eating in silence.

Most people have a meal or two in their back pocket for when they find themselves solo at the dinner table. It could be a bowl of cereal or a quick pasta dish. Some people, like my mother, will go all out on Friday nights and make pizza from scratch and pop a bottle of wine to enjoy with whatever she is watching on Netflix. I often find myself working late, so when I come home and have to prepare something for myself, I do not always have the energy or the enthusiasm to cook. I am more interested in assembling a vinegary salad or perhaps a quick dish of Butter Beans in Salsa Verde (page 29) with Olive Oil Fried Bread (page 42) and hot chilies or a can of tuna on the side. I rarely sit to eat when I am alone, but I will always use a cloth napkin, which I suppose is a nod to my sense that eating alone should be full of pleasure and enjoyed.

I do, in fact, refer to the foods I lean toward on my quiet, comforting evenings as belonging in their own category of Private Snacks. Some of the foods in this category certainly could be served to or with others, but often they are a bit messy, a bit over the top, or even a bit weird, and I like them best when I am standing, or maybe sitting on the counter, enjoying them on my own. Here is a brief list of my favourite Private Snacks for you to enjoy.

### Prosciutto Chips

This is exactly what it sounds like. You need about eight good-sized sturdy, plain potato chips. (I like Miss Vickie's, but who am I to tell you which chip to love the most?) Take four slices of prosciutto and tear them in half, lengthwise. Fold each piece of prosciutto and lay it on a chip. Arrange on your best china plate and eat.

### Messy Toast

Make a batch of Double Toasted Toaster Toast (page 42) using sourdough bread. Thickly spread a layer of Feta Cream (page 294), ricotta, Boursin, or basically anything creamy and delicious on the toast. Place a layer of thinly sliced hot sopressatta on the creamy layer. Spoon 1 to 2 tablespoons (15 to 30 mL) from a jar of prepared fire-roasted eggplant on the meat. Top with a lot of arugula and drizzle with Chili Crisp (page 288) and Hot Honey (page 293). Eat standing over a trashcan with a roll of paper towels wedged under your arm.

### Pepperoncini Butter Bread

Cut about four slices of fresh baguette. Thickly butter each slice with unsalted and, if possible, cultured butter. Put a pepperoncini on top of the butter. Eat immediately.

### Cold Roast Chicken

The day after you have roasted a Hot Honey Roast Chicken (page 210), pull it out of the fridge and set it on the counter. Sit or stand next to the chicken and pick off all the pieces you like best and eat them.

### Ice Cream

As with chips, I don't like to recommend an exact brand of ice cream because I'm pretty sure you already have a preferred brand, flavour, and texture. By all means, I encourage you, in your own Private Snacking, to be as *you* as you can possibly be. That said, my preferred ice cream experience is to have one large scoop of Häagen Dazs Caramel Cone Explosion (and yes, I definitely dig around to get as many chunks as possible when I'm dishing this out) *combined with* an additional scoop of Ben & Jerry's Chocolate Chip Cookie Dough in my favourite ceramic mug. For me, cacao nibs are the adult version of chocolate sprinkles, so I sprinkle these liberally on top of the ice cream along with a little flakey salt. This is best eaten in a comfy spot like a chair or a bed.

### Dutch Baby

Recipe follows (page 261).

# Dutch Baby with Berries and Crème Fraîche

**Serves 4**

### Crème Fraîche

½ cup (125 mL) heavy (35%) cream

1 tablespoon (15 mL) icing sugar

½ cup (125 mL) crème fraîche

### Dutch Baby

1 cup minus 1 tablespoon (235 mL) all-purpose flour

Pinch of salt

1 teaspoon (5 mL) icing sugar

5 large eggs

1 teaspoon (5 mL) pure vanilla extract

1 cup (250 mL) whole milk (3.25%) or nut milk

2 tablespoons (30 mL) unsalted butter, melted

1 tablespoon (15 mL) neutral oil, such as canola or grapeseed

### To serve

1 cup (250 mL) mixed fresh berries, such as blackberries and blueberries

1 tablespoon (15 mL) icing sugar

Maple syrup, for drizzling

A Dutch baby is essentially a giant puffy cross between a popover and a pancake. I love them, not just because they are quick to make and exciting to watch through the oven door, but because somehow they appeal deeply to my inner child. It could be the pancakey poof of the Dutch baby itself, the jumble of delicious berries, or even the icing sugar, but it's probably the drizzle of maple, which takes me right back to the winter of 1993 when my dad decided to tap the dozen or so maple trees in our backyard and spend hours filling the house with maple-scented fog as he reduced gallons of sap into a few jars of dark, sweet syrup. I remember it being a fun project, but not one without its challenges. After all, we did have to use the stove for other things. This recipe is so simple, so delicious, and tree-tapping is totally optional.

**Make the Crème Fraîche:** Place the bowl of a stand mixer in the freezer for 5 minutes to chill.

Place the cream and sugar in the chilled bowl of a stand mixer fitted with the whisk attachment. Whip to soft peaks. Remove the bowl from the mixer. Using a rubber spatula, fold in the crème fraîche until just combined. It's okay if it's a bit streaky. You don't want to mix it so much that the cream deflates. Cover and refrigerate until ready to serve.

**Make the Dutch Baby:** Preheat the oven to 475°F (240°C). Place a large cast iron skillet in the oven.

Place the flour, salt, sugar, eggs, vanilla, milk, and butter in a high-speed blender. Purée until smooth.

Remove the cast iron skillet from the oven. Add the oil and swirl it around so that the pan is evenly coated. Pour the batter into the skillet. Bake for 18 minutes, until golden brown and puffy. Carefully remove from the oven.

**To serve:** Immediately top the Dutch baby with the berries and dust it with the icing sugar. Spoon on as much crème fraîche and maple syrup as you like but be sure to put out more for people who might like a bit extra.

# Pear Cake

**Makes one 9-inch (23 cm) round cake**

¾ cup (175 mL) + 1 tablespoon (15 mL) granulated sugar, divided

¾ cup (175 mL) extra-virgin olive oil or good-quality canola oil

3 large eggs

Zest of 1 lemon

1 teaspoon (5 mL) salt

½ teaspoon (2 mL) ground nutmeg

1 cup (250 mL) all-purpose flour

2 teaspoons (10 mL) baking powder

4 small ripe Red Anjou or Bosc pears, halved and cored

Vanilla ice cream, to serve (optional)

This pear cake is very easy to make and also quite beautiful in its simplicity. You can, of course, add a scoop of vanilla ice cream or a cloud of just barely sweetened whipped cream, but it's also wonderful on its own, at ambient temperature or even chilled, as part of a mid-afternoon coffee klatsch with a good friend.

Preheat the oven to 350°F (180°C). Butter a 9-inch (23 cm) round cake pan.

In a medium bowl, whisk together ¾ cup (175 mL) of the sugar and the olive oil. Add the eggs, one at a time, beating well with a rubber spatula after each addition. Add the lemon zest, salt, and nutmeg. Stir to combine. Sift in the flour and baking powder. Stir until just combined.

Transfer the batter to the prepared pan. Use a spatula to spread it in an even layer. Place the pears, cut side up, in the batter, but don't press them in more than about ½ inch (1 cm), as the batter will rise as it bakes. Sprinkle the remaining 1 tablespoon (15 mL) of sugar on top. Bake for 30 to 32 minutes, until golden brown and a toothpick inserted into the centre comes out clean. Let cool in the pan for a few minutes before serving.

Cut the cake into squares and serve with a scoop of vanilla ice cream, if desired.

Store leftovers in an airtight container in the fridge for up to 4 days.

# Plum and Black Pepper Clafoutis

**Makes one 13- × 9-inch (3.5 L) clafoutis**

1 pound (450 g) ripe plums, halved and pitted

2 tablespoons (30 mL) dry red wine

1 tablespoon (15 mL) + 3 tablespoons (45 mL) icing sugar, divided, more for dusting

Cracked black pepper

5 large eggs

4 tablespoons (60 mL) heavy (35%) cream

2 tablespoons (30 mL) all-purpose flour

Pinch of salt

1 teaspoon (5 mL) pure vanilla extract

Sometimes I actually flip the script and make this for my daughters for breakfast. It's eggy and fruity and a touch sweet and comes together so quickly. Inspired by Julia Child's recipe for clafoutis, this version macerates the plums in red wine and black pepper and, true to my style, everything else gets chucked in the blender.

Place the plums, wine, and 1 tablespoon (15 mL) of the sugar in a large bowl. Add about 5 coarse grinds of pepper. Let sit for about 15 minutes, stirring once or twice if you think of it.

Preheat the oven to 425°F (220°C). Lightly grease a 13- × 9-inch (3.5 L) baking dish.

Place the remaining 3 tablespoons (45 mL) sugar, eggs, cream, flour, salt, and vanilla in a high-speed blender. Purée until smooth.

Pour just enough of the batter into the prepared baking dish to create a thin skin on the bottom. Bake for 30 seconds to 1 minute, until just set. Arrange the plums on top, reserving the macerating liquid. Pour the rest of the batter over the plums and return the dish to the oven. Bake for 18 to 20 minutes, until golden brown and puffy.

Dust with icing sugar and serve immediately with a splash of the macerating liquid on top.

Store leftovers in an airtight container in the fridge for up to 3 days.

# Apple Tart with Rose Cream

**Makes one 10-inch (25 cm) tart**

### Crust

½ cup (125 g) unsalted butter

1½ cups (375 mL) all-purpose flour, more for dusting

Pinch of salt

1 tablespoon (15 mL) granulated sugar

1 large egg, beaten

1 teaspoon (5 mL) white vinegar

2 tablespoons (30 mL) ice water, more if needed

### Filling

½ cup (125 mL) mascarpone cheese

2 tablespoons (30 mL) heavy (35%) cream

1 tablespoon (15 mL) icing sugar

3 to 4 Pink Lady apples, thinly sliced

1 large egg yolk, beaten

Turbinado sugar, for sprinkling

### Glaze

½ cup (125 mL) rose jam

2 tablespoons (30 mL) water

### Whipped Cream

1 cup (250 mL) heavy (35%) cream

Pinch of icing sugar

Splash of rose water

If you cut into the right apple, it will smell exactly like a rose. I try to re-create that moment in this recipe by splashing a little rose water into the whipped cream served with the pie. The combination makes this dish feel both playful and grown-up at the same time. It's sort of like an adult Passion Flakie, which is a nostalgia grocery store dessert from the mid-1990s that I don't think gets as much recognition as it should. Like a Passion Flakie, this tart has a flakey crust, a creamy layer, jam, and fruit—what could be more appealing at any age? I definitely would not trade this tart for Dunkaroos. You can find rose jam at most Middle Eastern grocery stores, but if you can't find it—no sweat—just use a seedless strawberry jam.

**Make the Crust:** Place the butter in the freezer for at least 20 minutes, or overnight.

Place the flour in a mound on a clean work surface, such as a counter or large cutting board. Sprinkle the salt and sugar overtop. Using your hand, make a well in the centre of the mound. Using the large holes of a box grater, grate the chilled butter into the well.

In a small bowl, whisk together the egg, vinegar, and ice water. Add it to the well. Using a dough knife, scoop the flour from the edges of the mound into the centre. Once the dough gets a bit sticky, flour your hands and knead briefly, until a dough forms, adding more flour if it's sticking to your hands or the work surface. Once you can form a ball, flatten it into a disc. Wrap tightly in plastic and chill in the fridge for at least 20 minutes.

Preheat the oven to 375°F (190°C). Line a rimmed baking sheet with parchment paper.

Sprinkle a clean work surface and a rolling pin with a bit of flour. Unwrap the chilled dough and set it before you. Using a firm grip, whack the dough disc a few times with the rolling pin to flatten it further. Roll out the dough into a circle about 12 inches (30 cm) in diameter. Carefully

*recipe continues*

transfer the dough to the prepared baking sheet.

**Make the Filling:** In a small bowl, combine the mascarpone, cream, and icing sugar. Using a spoon, dollop the mixture into the centre of the crust and smooth it out into a rough circle, leaving a 3-inch (8 cm) border around the edge of the pie. Place the apple slices on top of the cream mixture. Once the apples are in a nice mound, pull up the edges of the tart, folding them over the cream mixture and fruit. Brush the edges with the egg yolk. Sprinkle the tart all over with turbinado sugar. Bake for 30 to 35 minutes until the crust is golden brown and the apples are tender.

**Meanwhile, Make the Glaze and Whipped Cream:** Place the bowl and whisk attachment of a stand mixer in the freezer to chill.

In a small saucepan over medium heat, whisk the jam and water until combined. Bring to a boil and then turn off the heat. Brush the glaze all over the apples as soon as the tart comes out of the oven.

Secure the whisk attachment to the stand mixer. Add the cream and sugar to the chilled bowl. Whisk until soft peaks form. Add the rose water and whisk briefly to combine. Chill until ready to serve.

Serve the tart warm or at room temperature with a dollop of the whipped cream on each plate. Serve extra whipped cream on the side.

Store leftovers in an airtight container in the fridge for up to 4 days.

# Marble Cake

**Makes one 8½- × 4½-inch (1.5 L) loaf**

### Cake

3 large eggs, separated
½ teaspoon (2 mL) cream of tartar
1 cup (250 mL) granulated sugar
½ pound (225 g) unsalted butter, at room temperature
Zest of 1 navel orange
1¾ cups (425 mL) all-purpose flour
1 teaspoon (5 mL) baking powder
½ teaspoon (2 mL) baking soda
½ teaspoon (5 mL) salt
1 cup (250 mL) full-fat sour cream
2 tablespoons (30 mL) black cocoa powder

### Glaze

¼ cup (60 mL) granulated sugar
¼ cup (60 mL) water
Juice of 1 medium navel orange

I find it very satisfying to make this cake. There's something about not quite knowing exactly how the inside will look that makes it exciting to cut into and eat. Using black cocoa powder adds depth of colour to the cocoa swirl and makes for a really striking presentation. You can use regular cocoa, but the colour contrast will not be as sharp. A hint of orange adds brightness to the cake and cuts through some of the richness from the cocoa. All in all, I think you will agree that it's as wonderful to eat as it is to make.

**Make the Cake:** Preheat the oven to 350°F (180°C). Line a standard loaf pan with parchment paper. Place a wire rack over a rimmed baking sheet.

In the bowl of a stand mixer fitted with the whisk attachment, beat the egg whites and cream of tartar on high speed for 1 to 2 minutes, until they form stiff peaks. Gently, so as not to knock out any air, transfer the egg white mixture to a small bowl. Set aside.

Don't bother to wash the bowl of the stand mixer but do swap out the whisk attachment for the paddle attachment. Add the sugar, butter, and orange zest to the bowl. (Be sure not to discard the orange. You can use its juice to make the glaze.) Beat on medium-high speed for 2 to 3 minutes, until light and fluffy. Add the egg yolks one at a time, beating well after each addition, until combined.

In a medium bowl, sift the flour, baking powder, and baking soda. Sprinkle in the salt and stir to combine. Add about half of this mixture to the bowl of the stand mixer. Mix on low speed, until just combined. Add half of the sour cream. Mix to combine. Repeat, adding the remaining flour mixture and sour cream. Remove the bowl from the stand mixer and, using a rubber spatula, mix again briefly to ensure that there aren't any pockets of flour at the bottom of the bowl.

*recipe continues*

Transfer about one third of the batter to a medium bowl and set aside. To the remaining two thirds of the batter, add about two thirds of the egg white mixture. Fold in the egg whites until just combined. To the smaller amount of batter, add the cocoa. Stir until combined. Add the remaining egg white mixture and fold them in until just combined.

In the prepared loaf pan, dollop about one third of the white batter, followed by about half of the cocoa batter. Repeat. It's okay if it looks haphazard and blobby at this point—it's supposed to! Top with the remaining white batter. Run a large metal spoon under hot water for 1 minute and dry it on a clean kitchen towel. Use it to smooth the top. This will, as my grandmother would say, "marbelize" the cake. Bake for 70 minutes, until a cake tester inserted into the centre comes out clean. Let cool in the pan for 10 minutes. Transfer the cake to the wire rack to cool completely.

**Make the Glaze:** In a small saucepan, combine the sugar and water. Bring to a boil over high heat. Reduce the heat to medium. Let simmer until the liquid is reduced by half, about 3 to 5 minutes. Remove the saucepan from the heat. Add the orange juice and stir to combine.

Using a toothpick or thin metal skewer, poke about 20 holes all over the warm cake. Don't be too fussy about it; the holes will disappear once the glaze is on, but you do want them more or less spread out so the glaze really penetrates the cake and adds flavour and moisture. Using a pastry brush, brush the glaze all over the cake. Let the cake cool completely before serving.

Store leftovers in an airtight container in the fridge for up to 5 days.

# Torte in a Hurry

**Makes one 8-inch (20 cm) round torte**

10 tablespoons (140 g) unsalted butter, softened, more for greasing the pan

5 ounces (140 g) bittersweet chocolate, roughly chopped

½ cup (125 mL) toasted hazelnuts, more to garnish (see Toasted Nuts, page 290)

¾ cup (175 mL) granulated sugar

⅔ cup (150 mL) cocoa powder, more for dusting the pan

½ teaspoon (2 mL) salt

4 large eggs

Flakey salt, to garnish (optional)

I love the idea of creating recipes that are effortlessly elegant—the sort of thing you can throw together for a casual dinner that makes you look polished, organized, and capable but requires little in the way of time and technique. You do have to use a double boiler to melt the chocolate and butter here, but that only takes a few moments. Once that's done, the mixture goes into a high-powered blender with the remaining ingredients and then into the oven. The result is a simple but luscious and dense chocolate torte that is best served cold. Because it is so rich, a little goes a long way. I like to serve it in small slices alongside really good coffee or even a glass of cold oat milk for my daughters.

Preheat the oven to 325°F (160°C). Using a pastry brush, grease an 8-inch (20 cm) springform pan evenly with butter. Sift about 1 tablespoon (15 mL) of cocoa overtop. Gently shake out the excess so the pan is covered evenly in a fine dusting of cocoa.

Fill a medium saucepan with a couple of inches of water. Bring the water to a boil over high heat and then reduce the temperature to low. Place the butter in a large heatproof bowl. Place the bowl on top of the saucepan, making sure that the bottom of the bowl does not come in contact with the water. If there is too much water in the saucepan, dump some out and set the bowl on top again. Melt the butter. Add the chocolate and stir until it is more or less melted (it doesn't have to be perfect because it's going in the blender shortly). Turn off the heat and set aside.

Meanwhile, place the hazelnuts and about half of the sugar in a high-speed blender. Pulse to break up the nuts. Unplug the blender and stir. Add the remaining sugar. Plug the blender back in and blend on high speed until the nuts are finely ground. Add the cocoa and salt. Pulse to combine.

*recipe continues*

Using a rubber spatula, scrape the contents of the double boiler into the blender. Blend on high speed to combine, stopping the blender and scraping down the sides of the blender as necessary. With the blender running, add the eggs one at a time, blending until fully combined.

Spread the batter evenly into the prepared pan. Bake for 15 minutes, until the batter looks almost set, but not quite. It will continue to firm up as it chills. Let cool to room temperature, then transfer the torte to the fridge to set, uncovered, for at least 60 minutes. Serve cold, garnished with a handful of chopped hazelnuts and a sprinkle of flakey salt (if using).

Store leftovers in an airtight container in the fridge for up to 5 days.

# Polenta Biscuits with Sweet Corn Cream and Strawberries

**Serves 6**

### Corn Cream

2 ears of ripe sweet corn, shucked

2 cups (500 mL) heavy (35%) cream

1 tablespoon (15 mL) icing sugar (optional)

### Biscuits

1½ cups (375 mL) all-purpose flour, more for dusting

1 tablespoon (15 mL) granulated sugar (see Tip)

4 teaspoons (20 mL) baking powder

1 teaspoon (5 mL) baking soda

1 teaspoon (5 mL) salt

½ cup (125 mL) fine ground cornmeal

½ cup (125 mL) unsalted butter, frozen

1 tablespoon (15 mL) apple cider vinegar

1 cup (250 mL) full-fat sour cream or plain yogurt

### Strawberries

4 cups (1 L) fresh strawberries, hulled and quartered

1 tablespoon (15 mL) granulated sugar

1 teaspoon (5 mL) cracked pink peppercorns

My favourite kind of edge is a crispy edge. Swapping out some of the flour for fine ground cornmeal in a traditional baking powder biscuit brings me to that edgy bliss point, but also makes the biscuits a bit more rustic. They are as good with cold butter and country ham as they are as a base for creamy things and fruit, so I always recommend doubling the biscuit recipe and freezing half. Pre-portioned biscuits can be baked from frozen on lazy Sunday mornings or for the kind of summer picnic you read about in a Jane Austen novel.

**Prepare the Corn Cream:** Chop the corn into 2-inch (5 cm) chunks. Place it in a small saucepan. Add the cream. Bring to a boil over high heat. Cover and turn off the heat. Let the cream steep for 30 minutes. Using a fine-mesh sieve, strain out the corn. Place the cream in the fridge to chill for at least 1 hour, along with the bowl and whisk attachment of a stand mixer.

Preheat the oven to 425°F (220°C).

**Make the Biscuits:** In a medium bowl, sift the flour, sugar, baking powder, and baking soda. Add the salt and cornmeal. Stir to combine. Using the large holes on a box grater, grate in the butter. Add the vinegar and sour cream. Stir to combine.

Liberally dust a large clean work surface, such as a countertop or a cutting board, with flour. Using floured hands, turn the dough out and knead until it is smooth. Using a rolling pin, flatten the dough into a large rectangle about 2 inches (5 cm) thick. Fold the dough in half, over itself. It should be half the size but twice the thickness. Flatten to 2 inches (5 cm) thick again. Repeat this process 4 or 5 times to yield a flakier biscuit, finishing with a rectangle 2 inches (5 cm) thick. Transfer it to a large baking sheet and place it in the freezer for 15 minutes.

*recipe continues*

Cut the dough into 6 equal squares. Arrange them on a non-stick baking sheet. Bake for 18 to 20 minutes, until the outside is golden brown. If baking from frozen, let the biscuits sit on the tray at room temperature for 10 minutes before baking and add 5 minutes to the cook time. Remove from the oven and let cool on a wire rack until ready to serve.

**Macerate the Strawberries and Whip the Corn Cream:** Place the strawberries in a medium bowl and sprinkle them with the sugar and peppercorns. Toss to coat evenly. Let stand for 15 to 30 minutes at room temperature.

Fit the stand mixer with the chilled whisk attachment. Place the prepared corn cream and sugar (if using) in the chilled mixer bowl. Whisk on low speed, slowly increasing the speed as the cream thickens. Continue whisking until medium stiff peaks form, about 1 minute. Refrigerate until ready to serve.

**Assemble the Dish:** Cut the biscuits in half the way you would if making a sandwich. Divide them among plates, placing them cut side up. Top with a dollop of corn cream, strawberries, some of the berry juice, and the other half of the biscuit, placing it cut side down.

Leftover biscuits are notorious for not being as good, but you can store them in an airtight container at room temperature for 1 to 2 days and rewarm them in a hot oven for a few moments to make them taste better. The corn cream and strawberries also grow less delicious with time. I suggest you do your best to eat them fresh.

**Tip:** *These are not a sweet biscuit. If you'd like them to be a bit sweeter, add an additional 1 tablespoon (15 mL) granulated sugar. Conversely, you can make these biscuits savoury by adding about ½ cup (125 mL) grated cheese and either ¼ cup (60 mL) chopped scallions or sautéed onions. I like to make a double batch of cheese biscuits, so I can portion, freeze, and then bake them off for my girls on busy mornings. You can do the same! Just let the frozen biscuits thaw for about 10 minutes on a baking sheet and bake them for an extra 5 minutes as instructed above.*

# Sweet Potato Bread Pudding

**Serves 8 to 10**

### Sweet Potato Loaf

2 medium sweet potatoes, halved

2 eggs

½ cup (125 mL) canola oil

1½ cups (375 mL) granulated sugar

2 tablespoons (30 mL) apple cider vinegar

2 cups + 2 tablespoons (530 mL) all-purpose flour

2 teaspoons (10 mL) baking powder

1 teaspoon (5 mL) baking soda

1 teaspoon (5 mL) ground cinnamon

½ teaspoon (2 mL) ground nutmeg

½ teaspoon (2 mL) ground ginger

1 teaspoon (5 mL) salt

### Bread Pudding

1 Sweet Potato Loaf (recipe above)

1 cup (250 mL) heavy (35%) cream

4 eggs

¼ cup (60 mL) pure maple syrup

Pinch of sea salt

½ cup (125 mL) toasted walnuts, roughly chopped (see Toasted Nuts, page 290)

As far as autumnal desserts go, I feel like pie is the queen because of its deep and long-standing friendship with turkey and, ipso facto, Thanksgiving. But I think there should be space for desserts other than pie when the leaves change and the sweaters come out of storage. This might be controversial, but I can only eat so much pie before I'd like something cakey again. This bread pudding scratches that itch. While it does require baking a loaf cake and then the actual bread pudding, neither recipe is particularly onerous. If you find yourself losing momentum halfway through this bread pudding journey, you can set your lovely sweet potato loaf aside for a day or two or simply eat it as is, with loads of cool butter and flakey salt and a hot black coffee. The bread pudding, when complete, is worth the effort and has all the custardy and cakey textures you'd hope for, with the good synergy of fall flavours, warming spices, and crunchy toasted nuts.

**Make the Sweet Potato Loaf:** Preheat the oven to 425°F (220°C). Line a rimmed baking sheet with parchment paper.

Place the potatoes on the prepared baking sheet, cut side down. Roast for 30 to 40 minutes, until the potatoes are easily pierced with a paring knife. Using tongs, transfer them to a cooling rack.

Once the potatoes are cool enough to handle, scoop the warm flesh out of the skin and place it in a high-speed blender. Purée until smooth. Measure out 1¾ cups (425 mL) of purée. Reserve any remaining purée for another use.

Reduce the oven temperature to 350°F (180°C). Line a loaf pan with parchment paper.

In a high-speed blender, purée the 1¾ cups (425 mL) of the sweet potato purée, eggs, oil, sugar, and vinegar until well combined. Transfer the mixture to a clean, large bowl.

*recipe continues*

In a large bowl, sift the flour, baking powder, baking soda, cinnamon, nutmeg, and ginger. Add the salt and stir briefly to combine. Add about half of the dry ingredients to the sweet potato mixture. Using a spatula, fold the dry ingredients into the wet ingredients until just combined. Add the remaining dry ingredients and fold again until just combined. Transfer the batter to the prepared loaf pan. Bake for 70 to 80 minutes, or until a knife or toothpick inserted into the centre comes out clean. Place the loaf pan on a wire rack to cool for 15 minutes. Gently remove the loaf from the pan and place it on the wire rack to cool completely.

**Make the Bread Pudding:** Preheat the oven to 350°F (180°C). Generously grease a 9-inch (2.5 L) square baking dish with butter or cooking spray. Tear or cut the sweet potato loaf into large cubes and set aside.

In a large bowl, whisk together the cream, eggs, maple syrup, and salt. Add the loaf cubes and walnuts. Toss to combine. Let sit for 10 minutes to soak. Toss again.

Dump the mixture into the prepared baking dish. Bake for 30 to 40 minutes, or until set. Let cool for 10 to 15 minutes before serving.

Store leftovers in an airtight container in the fridge for up to 5 days.

# Lemon Meringue Fantasy

**Serves 8 to 10**

### Meringues
4 egg whites
Pinch of cream of tartar
½ cup (125 mL) granulated sugar

### Lemon Curd
1 cup (250 mL) granulated sugar
Zest and juice of 2 lemons
2 large eggs, beaten
2 large egg yolks, beaten
¼ cup (60 mL) cold unsalted butter, cut into cubes

4 cups (1 L) vanilla ice cream, softened

My mom snipped this recipe out of a *Gourmet* magazine in the 1990s, and it made appearances throughout my childhood. It is one of my favourites and is often the sweet spot at the end of the meal when I'm hosting a crowd. If you've never made meringues before, they can seem intimidating, but they really aren't. In this application—sandwiched between layers of vanilla ice cream and puddles of really lemony lemon curd— if they aren't perfectly round or they crack a bit, no one will notice. Be sure to separate your eggs when they are cold and then let them come to room temperature. This will ensure that they get as fluffy as possible.

**Make the Meringues:** Preheat the oven to 250°F (120°C). Line 2 baking sheets with parchment paper. Trace 2 circles, each about 8 inches (20 cm) in diameter, onto the parchment paper of the first sheet tray. Flip the parchment paper over so you can still see the circle outlines. On the second sheet, trace just one 8-inch (20 cm) circle. Flip the parchment paper over.

Place the egg whites in the bowl of a stand mixer fitted with the whisk attachment. Starting on low speed and increasing the speed gradually, whip the egg whites until soft peaks form. Add the cream of tartar. With the mixer on high speed, slowly add the sugar about 1 tablespoon (15 mL) at a time, until all the sugar has been added and the meringue is stiff and glossy.

Using a large spoon, divide the meringue evenly among the 3 circles you traced on the parchment paper. Smooth the tops so that they are more or less level. Bake for 50 to 60 minutes, until golden brown. Turn off the oven. Let the meringues cool in the oven until ready to assemble the dessert. If you need the oven in that time, set them on a wire rack on the counter to continue to dry out.

*recipe continues*

**Make the Lemon Curd:** In a medium saucepan, bring 2 inches (5 cm) of water to a simmer. In a large heatproof bowl, whisk together the sugar, lemon zest and juice, eggs, and yolks until combined. Place the bowl over the saucepan, ensuring that it does not touch the water, to create a double boiler. Using a heatproof spatula, stir continuously for 7 to 10 minutes, until the mixture becomes thick and glossy.

Carefully remove the bowl from the heat (there's a lot of hot steam under there). Using a fine-mesh sieve, strain the curd into a medium bowl. Drop in the butter, one cube at a time, stirring to incorporate it fully before adding the next cube.

Transfer the lemon curd to an airtight container. Let set in the fridge for 2 hours. Store it in the fridge for up to 2 weeks.

**Assemble the Dessert:** Select the best-looking meringue disc and set aside. You will use this for the top of the stack. Lay out the other 2 meringues on an inverted baking sheet. Divide the ice cream between the 2 meringues and, using an offset spatula, smooth out the top so that it is level. Place the baking sheet in the freezer and let the ice cream freeze completely. Remove the baking sheet from the freezer. Spoon the lemon curd on top of the ice cream, dividing it evenly between the 2 meringues. Working quickly, stack the 2 meringues on top of each other. Finish the stack with the remaining meringue. Return to the freezer until ready to serve.

Store leftovers in an airtight container in the freezer for up to 2 weeks.

# Condiments and Other Necessary Recipes

**Something to dip, spread, drizzle, dollop, schmear, or sprinkle doesn't just add to a dish, it completes it.**

Getting good food on the table for yourself regularly is an act of self-love. It involves a kind of care that I want to teach my daughters and that I want to share with the people around me. The food itself is a big part of it, but so is how you prepare it—the steps you invest time in, and where you cut corners. You could also spend the time you put into a meal elsewhere. Having a fridge full of smart condiments is one of the ways I save time without diminishing the effort I've put in. I've included my favourite recipes in this section.

In the spirit of my overall slap-dash attitude, however, I don't want you to get too caught up in making everything from scratch. If you can find a great hot honey or chili crisp, go ahead and buy it. It's fun to try different versions of your favourite condiments. I, for one, will never say no to a batch of someone else's homemade hot sauce. Always dip a clean spoon into your condiments and, just like any ingredient, rotate them regularly.

# Garlic Confit

**Makes about 2 cups (500 mL)**

½ pound (225 g) peeled garlic cloves
2 to 3 red bird's eye chilies
1½ cups (375 mL) extra-virgin
   olive oil

I love garlic, but I hate chopping it. It always gets stuck to the knife and smells up my hands and generally annoys me when I'm peeling it. I used to smash garlic cloves and add them to whatever I was cooking, but then every once in a while I'd end up eating an entire garlic clove. To me, that felt like finding a prize, but I believe it also made other people wary of my cooking. Preparing garlic confit in batches means I only have to peel a bunch of garlic once (or you can really treat yourself and buy pre-peeled garlic; there is no shame in that), and that the flavour and texture of the garlic is mellow enough so that biting into it is less jarring. The confit oil is also delicious and great for drizzling on veggies, bread, soups, salads, or basically anything you think could be enhanced by a drizzle.

In a small saucepan over medium-high heat, bring the garlic, chilies, and olive oil to just barely a simmer. Reduce the heat to low. Cook the confit, stirring occasionally, for about 30 minutes, or until the garlic is tender and easily pierced with a paring knife.

Using a slotted spoon, transfer the garlic to a clean 16-ounce (500 mL) jar with a tight fitting lid. Pour the oil overtop. Refrigerate immediately.

Store the garlic confit in an airtight container in the fridge for up to 3 weeks. Because garlic is such a low-acid vegetable, when it's preserved it needs to be kept in the fridge. If you want to keep the garlic confit for longer than a few weeks, you can freeze it and use as normal.

# Crispy Shallots

**Makes about 1 cup (250 mL)**

4 to 6 medium shallots, thinly sliced
1 cup (250 mL) neutral oil, such as
canola or grapeseed
Salt

Crispy shallots are like an onion and a bread crumb combined, which means they make everything more delicious and crunchier—and who doesn't want that? Tossed on salads, sprinkled onto noodles, even scattered onto roast fish with a handful of herbs and lots of lime, put them anywhere you want a little something extra. You do have to use quite a bit of oil to make these, but afterwards I strain the oil, cool it, and either use it to make dressings or whip it into a garlicky aioli for dipping and schmearing. If this all seems like too much effort, check your local Middle Eastern grocery store for pre-crisped onions—they are also a great option.

Line a large plate with paper towels.

Place the shallots and oil in a medium saucepan over high heat. Cook, stirring occasionally, for 15 to 20 minutes, until they are golden brown and crispy. Using a slotted spoon, carefully transfer the shallots to the prepared plate. Sprinkle with salt. Let cool.

Cool the oil and place it in an airtight container in the fridge for future use. Once the shallots have cooled, store them in an airtight container at room temperature for up to 5 days until ready to use.

# Chili Crisp

**Makes about 2 cups (500 mL)**

10 shallots, thinly sliced
  (about 2 cups/500 mL)

1 head of garlic, thinly sliced

1½ cups (375 mL) neutral oil,
  such as canola or grapeseed

1 tablespoon (15 mL) granulated sugar

1 tablespoon (15 mL) sesame oil

1 tablespoon (15 mL) white vinegar

2 tablespoons (30 mL) dark soy sauce

2 teaspoons (10 mL) dried Szechuan
  peppercorns

¼ cup (60 mL) dried red chili flakes

Not only is this homemade version always in my fridge, but I also have at least a half a dozen different brands of chili crisp taking up space. I was introduced to this wonder condiment years ago when I lived in Flushing, in Queens, New York. I grabbed a jar of Lao Gan Ma at a local grocery store, not really knowing what it was but intrigued by the contents of the jar. It was crunchy, spicy, and full of umami, and it's great on everything from dumplings to vanilla ice cream (really). There are so many great brands, and where I live there are amazing locally made options like Cheng Du, Okazu, and Zing, but I also like making my own. It allows me the flexibility to toggle the sweetness and acidity up and down. If you're looking for Szechuan peppercorns, they can be a bit tricky to find, but you can usually source them in your local Chinatown or at a bulk food store like Bulk Barn.

Line a large plate with paper towels. Set a fine-mesh sieve over a large metal bowl.

In a medium saucepan over medium heat, place the shallots, garlic, and oil and cook for about 15 minutes until the shallots are golden brown and crispy. Dump the mixture through the sieve so that the oil is drained off the shallots and garlic into the metal bowl. Place the sieve on the prepared plate to allow the shallots and garlic to dry and crisp further.

Whisk the sugar, sesame oil, vinegar, soy sauce, peppercorns, and chili flakes into the hot oil and let cool to room temperature. Return the crispy shallots and garlic to the oil mixture. Transfer everything to an airtight container.

Store chili crisp in the fridge for up to 1 month.

# Bread Crumbs

**Makes about 1 cup (250 mL)**

2 cups (500 mL) stale bread crusts, slices, and baguette ends

1 tablespoon (15 mL) extra-virgin olive oil

Salt

Homemade bread crumbs are one of the most low-effort, high-impact ingredients I can think of. You can make them very fine or so large they are basically a crouton. My favourite approach is to Goldilocks the whole effort and make them various sizes in between. Then you can strew (yes, strew!) these lovely crunchy bits on top of a salad, pasta, a casserole, some kind of roasted vegetable situation—anywhere! Your life will only be improved by making bread crumbs at home, so please give it a go.

Preheat the oven to 325°F (160°C). Line a rimmed baking sheet with parchment paper.

Chop the bread into large chunks. Arrange it in a single layer on the prepared baking sheet. Drizzle with the olive oil. Sprinkle with salt to taste.

Bake for 10 to 15 minutes, until golden brown. Remove from the oven and let cool for 5 to 10 minutes.

Transfer the toasted bread to a cutting board and chop until you achieve your desired crumb size. If you like, you can also chuck the toasted bread in a blender and pulse to create crumbs, but please note that you will not have as much control over their size.

Use immediately or store the bread crumbs in an airtight container in the freezer for up to 1 month.

# Toasted Nuts

2 cups (500 mL) shelled raw nuts, such as hazelnuts, walnuts, or pistachios

I don't think a nut exists that doesn't benefit from a quick ride in the oven. Toasting nuts intensifies their flavour and dries them out *just a touch* so that they grow a little more delicious and a little crunchier as well. It's a small thing that makes a big difference, and so I do recommend, if you have the time and the oven space—and most importantly the inclination—that you toast your nuts. What follows is less a recipe and more of a loose method, since the nut you choose will determine your exact toasting time. If you want to toast a few different nuts together, make sure they are all the same general size or else their toasting times will be different.

Preheat the oven to 325°F (160°C). Line a baking sheet with parchment paper.

Spread the nuts in an even layer on the prepared baking sheet. Bake for 8 minutes (or 6 minutes if they are very small nuts like pine nuts). Remove the baking sheet from the oven, give the nuts a stir, and check to see if they are golden and smell nuttier than they did before they went in the oven. You're going to have to use your judgment here, but I find 8 minutes to be a good amount of time for a light toast on a medium-size nut. For a darker toast, or a larger nut, return to the oven for 2 to 4 minutes and then check again. Repeat as necessary, until your nuts are perfectly golden brown. Let cool.

Store the toasted nuts in an airtight container in the fridge for up to 2 weeks.

# Two Pickles

There are two pickles that I always have on hand not just because they are delicious and I reach for them often, but also because I often find myself splashing the brine they are packed in onto a salad or drizzling it over a piece of fish.

## Bread and Butter Pickles

**Makes one 4-cup (1 L) jar of pickles**

12 mini cucumbers
2 tablespoons (30 mL) salt, divided
1 cup (250 mL) granulated sugar
1¼ cups (300 mL) white vinegar
2 teaspoons (10 mL) yellow mustard seeds
1 teaspoon (5 mL) fennel seeds
½ teaspoon (2 mL) turmeric powder
½ teaspoon (2 mL) celery seeds

Rinse the cucumbers and shake off any excess water. Cut the cucumbers into ½-inch (1 cm) slices. Toss with 1 tablespoon (15 mL) of the salt. Place the cucumbers in a large colander to drain.

Meanwhile, in a small saucepan over high heat, combine the remaining 1 tablespoon (15 mL) salt, the sugar, vinegar, mustard seeds, fennel seeds, turmeric, and celery seeds. Bring to a boil, stirring occasionally until the sugar and salt dissolve. When the mixture boils, remove it from the heat and set aside to cool.

Briefly rinse the cucumbers to remove any excess salt. Place them in a large 4-cup (1 L) mason jar with a lid. Once the brine has cooled, pour it over the cucumbers so that they are fully submerged. Screw the lid tightly on the jar. Place the jar of pickles in the fridge, upside down, and let it rest overnight before eating. These pickles can be kept refrigerated for up to 2 weeks.

## Pickled Chilies

**Makes one 4-cup (1 L) jar of pickles**

4 cups (1 L) red long chilies
1 cup (250 mL) granulated sugar
1 cup (250 mL) white vinegar

Rinse the chilies. Trim off the stems and slice them as thinly as possible. Place the chilies in a large 4-cup (1 L) mason jar with a lid.

Meanwhile, in a small saucepan over high heat, combine the sugar and vinegar. Bring to a boil, stirring occasionally, until the sugar dissolves.

Pour the hot brine over the chilies. Let stand on the counter, uncovered, for about 1 hour. Screw the lid tightly on the jar and store in the fridge for up to 2 weeks.

# Hot Vinegar

**Makes about 4 cups (1 L)**

4 cloves garlic, smashed
1 cup (250 mL) assorted fresh chilies, such as jalapeno, Fresno, and green
3½ cups (875 mL) white vinegar
1 tablespoon (15 mL) granulated sugar

This is an easy and quick condiment to make at the end of summer when gardens are overflowing with peppers. The longer it sits, the spicier it gets, so have a taste before you go splashing it on your oysters (page 21).

Place the garlic and chilies in a 32-ounce (950 mL) glass jar with a tight-fitting lid.

In a medium saucepan over high heat, whisk together the vinegar and sugar until the sugar dissolves. Bring the mixture just to a boil, then turn off the heat. Pour the vinegar over the chilies and garlic. Let cool to room temperature. Cover and store in the fridge until ready to use.

If you use a clean utensil when dipping into the hot vinegar, it will keep in the refrigerator indefinitely.

# Hot Honey

**Makes about 1 cup (250 mL)**

1 cup (250 mL) pure liquid honey
1 tablespoon (15 mL) white vinegar
2 to 3 long red chilies, halved lengthwise
1 teaspoon (5 mL) dried red chili flakes
1 teaspoon (5 mL) Aleppo pepper
Pinch of salt

Hot honey is one of those things I can't believe I ever lived without. It's such an easy thing to put together, and it adds so much to any dish. Drizzle it over Baked Cheese (page 45) or Fried Cabbage with Halloumi and Jalapenos (page 151), or level up your takeout fried chicken (heck, it's pretty great on a McNugget!), a buttered biscuit, or even a simple platter of roast veggies.

In a small saucepan over medium-high heat, combine all the ingredients. Bring the mixture to a simmer, then remove the saucepan from the heat. Let cool to room temperature.

If you prefer a smooth hot honey, use a fine-mesh sieve to strain out the solids as you transfer the honey to a 16-ounce (500 mL) jar with a tight-fitting lid. Store in the refrigerator until ready to use.

If you use a clean spoon when dipping into the hot honey, it will keep in the refrigerator indefinitely.

# Tahini Dip

**Makes about 2 cups (500 mL)**

1 cup (250 mL) tahini
Juice of 1 lemon
½ teaspoon (2 mL) salt, more to taste
⅞ cup (200 mL) ice water

I could eat this dip on anything, and it's so quick to make. It's just sesame paste blended with loads of cold water and a bit of salt and lemon. After you whip it in your blender, it becomes unbelievably light and smooth. I like to slather it on pita bread, but it also makes a great "creamy situation" to schmear on a large plate and plunk roasted vegetables or fresh salads onto. It is also a great swap for Feta Cream (page 294) in dishes like Crispy Eggplant with Spicy Vinaigrette (page 145) and Roasted Beet and Socca Tart (page 157).

Place the tahini, lemon juice, and salt in a high-speed blender. Pulse a few times to combine. With the blender running on high, slowly stream in the ice water until fully combined. The tahini dip should be pale and thick. Season with salt to taste.

Use immediately or store in an airtight container in the fridge for up to 1 week. The dip will get a touch firmer as it cools.

# Feta Cream

**Makes about 2 cups (500 mL)**

8 ounces (225 g) feta cheese
    (Macedonian is best), plus
    1 tablespoon (15 mL) brine
½ cup (125 mL) heavy (35%) cream
1 tablespoon (15 mL) extra-virgin
    olive oil

Dip, dressing, schmear—this is whatever you want it to be, and it's great wherever you put it. I spread it on crackers, layer it under Crispy Eggplant with Spicy Vinaigrette (page 145), or dollop it on grilled vegetables.

Place all the ingredients in a high-speed blender. Purée until smooth.

Store in an airtight container in the fridge for up to 1 week.

# Aioli

**Makes 1½ cups (375 mL)**

2 cloves Garlic Confit (page 286), plus 1 tablespoon (15 mL) of its oil

1 large egg

1 large egg yolk

1 tablespoon (15 mL) Dijon mustard

Zest and juice of 1 lemon

1 cup (250 mL) neutral oil, such as canola or grapeseed

½ cup (125 mL) extra-virgin olive oil

Salt

Aioli, or mayonnaise, is not difficult to prepare, but using a homemade version makes a world of difference in terms of taste. It's great as a spread on sandwiches and pitas, but also works as a dip for fresh veggies or the base of a salad dressing. Use the freshest eggs you can find, and choose a good quality neutral oil that doesn't have a strong flavour.

In a high-speed blender, pulse the garlic and its oil, the egg, egg yolk, Dijon, and lemon zest and juice until smooth.

With the blender running on low, slowly stream in the oil. Continue blending until the oil fully is incorporated and the aioli has become pale and thick. Add salt, to taste. Pulse to combine.

Store aioli in an airtight container in the fridge for up to 1 week.

# Tartar Sauce

**Makes 1½ cups (375 mL)**

1 cup (250 mL) Aioli (page 295) or prepared mayonnaise

½ cup (125 mL) chopped dill pickles

1 tablespoon (15 mL) chopped capers, plus 1 tablespoon (15 mL) of their juice

1 tablespoon (15 mL) chopped fresh dill

1 tablespoon (15 mL) chopped preserved lemon (optional)

Pinch of sugar (optional)

Tartar Sauce is typically associated with fish dishes, but I put it just about anywhere I am looking for a hit of creamy acidity. I'll spread it on burgers, dollop it on roasted veggies and even use it as a key ingredient in Every Night Salad (page 53). If you don't feel like making Aioli (page 295), no sweat. Just use a full-fat prepared mayonnaise that appeals to you.

Place all of the ingredients in a medium bowl. Stir to combine.

Store leftovers in an airtight container in the fridge for up to 1 week.

# Harissa

**Makes about 2 cups (500 mL)**

7 guajillo chilies
1 ancho chili
2 bird's eye chilies, stems removed
2 cloves garlic, smashed
2 teaspoons (10 mL) cumin seeds
2 teaspoons (10 mL) coriander seed
2 teaspoons (10 mL) kosher salt
2 teaspoons (10 mL) sweet paprika
1 teaspoon (5 mL) Aleppo pepper
1 teaspoon (5 mL) granulated sugar
1 tablespoon (15 mL) white vinegar
1 cup (250 mL) neutral oil, such as
   canola or grapeseed

I make this condiment regularly, and I always prepare a double batch because it is a great add-on to so many different dishes. Whenever I'm looking for dinner inspiration, I haul this harissa out first and think about what's in my fridge. What can I schmear, rub, dollop, or drizzle it on? With some harissa in my back pocket, I am able to create something delicious with minimal time and effort. Depending on how much you blend this, it can become quite creamy. I like to pulse the oil in so that the paste and the oil remain separate and can be used as two different ingredients—a highly seasoned chili paste and a spicy, beautiful finishing oil.

Place the guajillo and ancho chilies in a medium bowl. Fill it with room-temperature water and let the chilies soak for 20 minutes. Remove the stems and as many of the seeds as you can from the soaked chilies (missing a few won't hurt). Place them in a high-speed blender. Add the bird's eye chilies, garlic, cumin, coriander, salt, paprika, Aleppo, sugar, and vinegar. Purée until smooth.

If you want the harissa to be creamy and emulsified, you can stream in the oil with the blender running on high speed and continue to blend until the oil is fully incorporated. If you're like me and prefer to keep some of the oil available for drizzling, add the oil all at once and pulse to combine.

Store in an airtight jar in the fridge for up to 1 week.

# Dukkah

**Makes about 1 cup (250 mL)**

2 tablespoons (30 mL) cumin seeds

2 tablespoons (30 mL) coriander seeds

1 tablespoon (15 mL) fennel seeds

2 teaspoons (10 mL) black peppercorns

⅔ cup (150 mL) toasted hazelnuts
(see Toasted Nuts, page 290)

⅓ cup (75 mL) toasted almonds
(see Toasted Nuts, page 290)

2 teaspoons (10 mL) salt

Dukkah is a blend of warm spices, seeds, and nuts traditional to Egypt. Although it's technically a spice mix, it has layers of flavour and texture and can be used simply as a dip with extra-virgin olive oil and bread or sprinkled on roasted veggies and meats, in salads, or on eggs.

In a small skillet over high heat, place the cumin, coriander, fennel, and peppercorns. Toast, shaking the skillet occasionally so that they do not burn, until they are fragrant and toasted, about 2 to 4 minutes. Remove from the heat immediately.

Transfer the spices to a high-speed blender. Pulse until finely ground. Add the hazelnuts, almonds, and salt. Pulse a few times to grind into a coarse meal. You don't want to pulse the nuts too much or you will make nut butter, which is delicious but not what you're looking for here.

Transfer the mixture to a 2-cup (500 mL) glass jar with a tight-fitting lid. Store it in the fridge until ready to use.

If you use a clean utensil when dipping into the dukkah, it will keep in the refrigerator indefinitely.

# Flatbread Dough

**Makes 2 large flatbreads,
roughly 11 × 8 inches
(28 × 20 cm) each**

1 tablespoon (15 mL) pure liquid honey
or granulated sugar

1 cup (250 mL) lukewarm water

1 tablespoon (15 mL) active dry yeast

2 cups (500 mL) all-purpose flour, more
for kneading

2 tablespoons (30 mL) extra-virgin
olive oil, more for the dough ball

1 teaspoon (5 mL) salt

There are some amazing longer-ferment, sourdough starter–based flatbread dough recipes out there, but this isn't one of them. If I decide I want toppings on a carb, whether in flatbread, pizza-esque, or even pita form, I'd like to be eating it by the end of the day. Also, despite my best intentions, I have killed every sourdough starter I have ever had, so here I present you with a user-friendly, commercial yeast–based flatbread dough recipe, from which endless variations are possible.

In a large bowl, mix the honey and lukewarm water until the honey is dissolved. Sprinkle in the yeast and let sit for 10 minutes, until the water is bubbly.

Using a wooden spoon, stir in 1 cup (250 mL) of the flour, the oil, and salt. Slowly add the remaining 1 cup (250 mL) flour to yield a kneadable dough.

Lightly flour a clean work surface. Flour your hands and turn the dough out. Knead for about 10 minutes. When it's ready, the dough will no longer be tacky and will feel like an earlobe.

Lightly oil a medium bowl and the dough ball. Place the dough in the bowl and cover with a clean kitchen towel. Let rise in a warm (but not hot) spot until the dough doubles in size, about 40 minutes. Punch down the dough.

If you are hoping to eat right away, lightly flour a clean work surface and roll the dough into 2 large rectangles, each roughly 11 × 8 inches (28 × 20 cm). If you want to save the dough for later, wrap it tightly in a zip top bag and store it in the fridge for up to 12 hours or in the freezer for up to 3 months. Just be sure to let frozen dough come back to room temperature before you roll it out.

Bake as directed for Garlic Fingers (page 46) or Zucchini and Feta Flatbread with Harissa and Pine Nuts (page 49). You can also try topping this flatbread with ingredients like tomato sauce, pesto, roasted veggies, leftovers, cheese, béchamel, etc. Bake in a 475°F (240°C) oven for 10 to 12 minutes, until the crust is golden brown and the toppings are hot and bubbling.

# Acknowledgements

What a long and strange journey it has been. This book was written, tested, styled, and shot during a strange and, at moments, overwhelming time and would not have been possible without the amazing team that put it together. Alyssa and Chris, Andy, and Lindsay—it is both a pleasure and a privilege to work alongside you. This book is better because of your work, and I look forward to a lifetime of collaborations with each of you.

Laura Dosky! You are truly, truly the best. You helped me get out of my own way, which is a feat in itself. The rest of the team at Penguin Canada: Andrea, Nicole, Michelle, Leah, and Matthew.

Ren, thanks for agreeing to join in the fun and for offering kind but firm guidance. Kasia and Jemimah, you made it a party at a time when parties were actually kind of banned. Thank you. Erica, I'm so glad you could be a part of this, especially the part where you managed to distract my children and calm me, all the while looking regal and composed in a polyester dress in 40°C weather. Shaniah and Nataschia your kindness gave me the time to do this, but also the support I needed to keep going.

Brilynn. Good grief, I put you through a lot. Mostly eating mapo tofu, but also having to deal with my endless self-doubt, second-guessing and fits of crying in your doorway. Thank you, thank you, thank you. Alan, you are so very special to me, thank you for your patience, your advice, and your hugs. Art, it's been nine years since we met in the aisle and I am grateful every day for your role in my life. Bas, always. Sherry, Bethany, Misha, Nikita and Aleks, Kris and Kyle, Kat and Stacey, Liza, Zach and Rosa, Charlotte, Rossy, and Hassel. Nico! I love you all. Zach, Seana and baby Wila, you are our forever bubble. Martin, we've come a long way. Thank you for supporting me.

Oscar, I could write a whole book of gratitude to you. I love you without limit.

Piper and Matilda, you are the first thing, and then the last. I am so very proud of the people you are. I want you to know I will always come to the table for you.

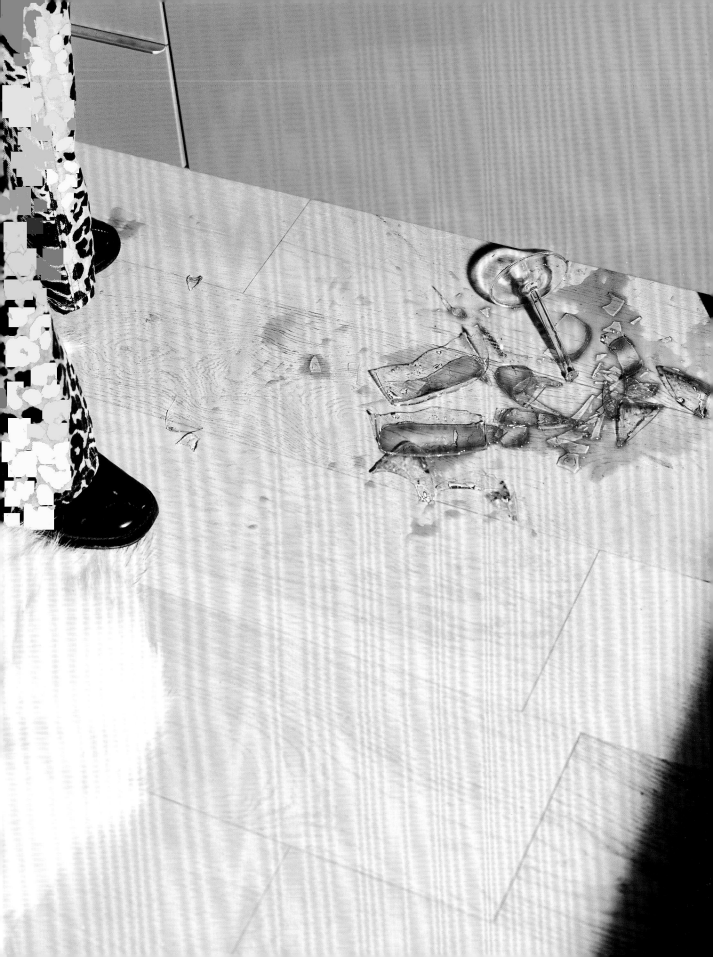

# Index